Christ in All of *Scripture*

A 52-WEEK JOURNEY OF DISCOVERING JESUS
ON EVERY PAGE OF THE BIBLE

Volume Three

This study belongs to:

_____

_____

THE DAILY GRACE CO.®

Christ in All of Scripture: A 52-Week Journey of Discovering Jesus on Every Page of the Bible | Volume 3
Copyright © 2024 by The Daily Grace Co.®
Spring, Texas. All rights reserved.

Unless otherwise noted, all Scripture quotations are taken from the Christian Standard Bible®, Copyright © 2020 by Holman Bible Publishers. Used by permission. Christian Standard Bible® and CSB® are federally registered trademarks of Holman Bible Publishers.

Scripture quotations marked NLT are taken from the Holy Bible, New Living Translation, copyright ©1996, 2004, 2015 by Tyndale House Foundation. Used by permission of Tyndale House Publishers, Carol Stream, Illinois 60188. All rights reserved.

Supplemental material: pages 12, 14–17, 206–207, and 215–217. Copyright © 2019 by The Daily Grace Co.®

Supplemental material: pages 8–10, 13, 204–205, 209–214, and 201–206. Copyright © 2024 by The Daily Grace Co.®

The extra on page 138 was originally published in *The Bible Handbook*. Copyright © 2020, 2024 by The Daily Grace Co.®

The Daily Grace Co.® exists to equip disciples to know and love God and His Word by creating beautiful, theologically rich, and accessible resources so that God may be glorified and the gospel made known.

Designed in the United States of America and printed in China.

God has been faithful, and because of His faithfulness, Israel can rejoice and have hope.

Table of Contents

INTRODUCTION

How to Use This Resource 8
Study Suggestions 12
How to Study the Bible 14
Timeline of Scripture 16

WEEK TWENTY-SEVEN 19
WEEK TWENTY-EIGHT 33
WEEK TWENTY-NINE 47
WEEK THIRTY 61
WEEK THIRTY-ONE 75
WEEK THIRTY-TWO 87
WEEK THIRTY-THREE 99
WEEK THIRTY-FOUR 111
WEEK THIRTY-FIVE 127
WEEK THIRTY-SIX 141
WEEK THIRTY-SEVEN 157
WEEK THIRTY-EIGHT 171
WEEK THIRTY-NINE 189

EXTRAS

Psalms of Lament 72
Israel as a Fruitless Vine 124
Messianic Prophecies in Isaiah 138
The Servant Songs of Isaiah 186
Appendix A:
   How to See Christ
      in All of Scripture 204
Appendix B:
   The Attributes of God 206
Appendix C:
   Annotation Examples and Tips 209
Appendix D:
   The Metanarrative of Scripture 215
What is the Gospel? 216

Introduction to
Christ in All of Scripture | Volume 3

You've made it to *Christ in All of Scripture: A 52-Week Journey of Discovering Jesus on Every Page of the Bible* | *Volume 3*!

As you continue in your study, remember that the Old Testament and New Testament tell one story, and they are far more intertwined than we sometimes realize. As we saw from the beginning of the first volume, that story begins in the Old Testament, and it contains numerous threads that run throughout and find their resolution in the New Testament. Because of this, we cannot fully appreciate the New Testament without also appreciating the Old—and vice versa.

And standing at the center of this one story that unites both testaments is Jesus Christ. He Himself is the main character and climax of the story that began in the Old Testament. For that reason, we can appropriately say that Jesus Christ is present in *all* of Scripture, not just a quarter of it.

Of course, it's easy to say that Jesus is in all of Scripture. But the study you hold in your hands will help you see it. And our prayer is that in seeing how He is present throughout the whole Bible, your love for Jesus and for His Word will grow.

> Standing at the center of this one story that unites both testaments is Jesus Christ.

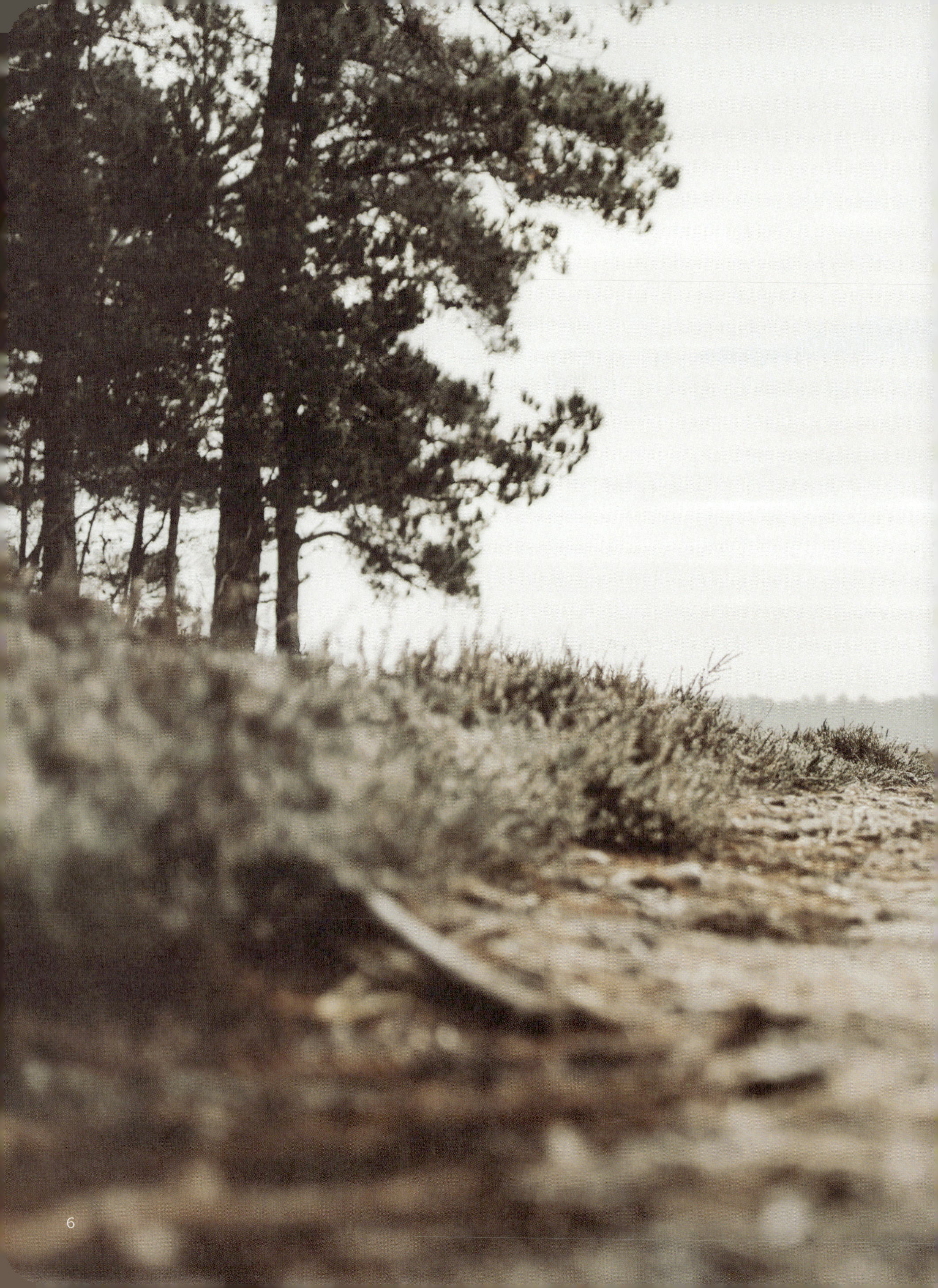

In seeing how He is present throughout the whole Bible, your love for Jesus and for His Word will grow.

How to Use This Resource

As our journey continues, this section provides reminders of some practical considerations that will help you make the most of this study.

IN THIS STUDY

This study is the third of four volumes in the *Christ in All of Scripture* study set from The Daily Grace Co.® Each volume covers roughly one quarter, or thirteen weeks, of content. And together, these four volumes were designed to be completed over the course of one calendar year—from January 1 through December 31.

> NOTE:
> *Visit www.thedailygraceco.com to purchase the other three volumes in this study set (Volumes 1, 2, and 4).*

Over the course of this year—just as we did in the first two volumes—we will continue walking through passages from most of the books of the Old Testament, showing how these passages ultimately point to Jesus. In this way, we will discover how Christ is truly present on every page and in every passage of Scripture.

WEEKLY RHYTHMS

The main content of this study starts in Week 27. There are five days of content for each week, so most readers will likely find it helpful to complete the study content on Mondays through Fridays. Then, the weekends can be used to catch up on any missed study days or to reflect on what you learned.

Each week in this volume contains the following elements:

> *Weekly Introduction*
> Each week will begin with a short introduction that will share the Old Testament and New Testament passages of Scripture we will study that week.

> *Days 1 and 3: "Mark it Up"*
> On Days 1 and 3, you will be asked to repetitively read and annotate our two weekly passages. If the idea of annotation seems overwhelming to you—perhaps something you have not done since high school English class—do not fret! We will provide helpful prompts to guide you along the way. You can also find some annotation examples on pages 209–214.

> These study days might initially seem quite short, especially compared to past Bible studies you may have completed, but we encourage you to make the most of this

step! The observations you make on Days 1 and 3—through the highlights, underlines, and notes you write in the margins—will guide the rest of your progress throughout the week.

Additionally, if you come across a prompt that challenges you or leaves you with more questions than answers, that's okay! You may find it helpful to look at the surrounding context of that passage (i.e., the verses or chapters that come just before and just after it). And at times, you may simply jot down your questions to come back to later in the week.

> *For annotation examples, as well as other helpful tips and tools for completing this study, see the Appendix, starting on page 203.*

Days 2 and 4: "Go Deeper" + "Make the Christ Connection"
On Days 2 and 4, you will find commentary that helps further explain and connect that week's passages of Scripture, as well as some questions that will help you more deeply consider what you have read and make connections of your own. We suggest you begin these days by rereading the passages. Then, give yourself plenty of time to read the commentary and answer the questions as you go deeper into each passage.

Day 5: "Live It Out"
Finally, the week will end with some intentional time to consider how you might apply what you have learned. This is an important step that will help you move from head knowledge to heart knowledge and then to actionable steps to live out the truths you have learned. We suggest you start Day 5 by reading that week's main passages of Scripture once more and then setting aside some time to pray and walk through the provided application questions as you consider how God might be calling you to respond.

Christ is truly present on every page and in every passage of Scripture.

Whether this is your first time completing a Bible study or you have been studying God's Word for decades, the unique weekly format of this study may still feel new and perhaps even challenging at first. If that's the case for you, don't forget to give yourself grace through the process and remember that God has not left you to study His Word on your own. If you are a believer, His Spirit dwells within you and will guide you as you approach Scripture.

AS YOU CONTINUE

Ready to keep going? As you continue in this yearlong journey, remember that the goal of this study is not perfection but growth in your understanding of God's Word. In other words, we do not expect you to annotate every passage or answer every question perfectly. Instead—day by day, week by week, and volume by volume—we pray that you would progressively grow in your ability to see Christ in all of Scripture. And as you do, we pray that you will grow to love Him and His Word more.

Jesus is the main character of the story. He is the One to whom all of Scripture points. And so, let us seek to magnify Him as we embark on the remaining weeks of study. To Him be the glory!

Jesus is the main character of the story. He is the One to whom all of Scripture points.

Study Suggestions

We believe that the Bible is true, trustworthy, and timeless and that it is vitally important for all believers. These study suggestions are intended to help you more effectively study Scripture as you seek to know and love God through His Word.

SUGGESTED STUDY TOOLS

- ☐ Bible
- ☐ Journal to write notes or prayers
- ☐ Pens, colored pencils, and highlighters
- ☐ Dictionary to look up unfamiliar words

Did you know that there is a podcast that goes along with this study?

A YEAR IN THE BIBLE
WITH DAILY GRACE®

Check out season 4 of *A Year in the Bible with Daily Grace* for encouragement as you complete this study—available wherever you listen to podcasts.

How to Study the Bible

The Inductive Method provides tools for deeper and more intentional Bible study. This study will guide you through the three steps of the Inductive Method listed below—equipping you to observe, interpret, and apply two passages of Scripture each week. In addition, the questions listed under each of the steps below can be used to aid your study of the weekly passages.

Weekly rhythm: On Days 1 and 3 of each week, we recommend referring to the "observation and comprehension" step and key question. On Days 2 and 4, we recommend following the "interpretation" step and key question. And on Day 5, we recommend referencing the "application" step and key question.

01 *Observation & Comprehension*
KEY QUESTION: WHAT DOES THE TEXT SAY?

After reading the daily Scripture in its entirety at least once, begin working with smaller portions of the Scripture. Read a passage of Scripture repetitively, and then mark the following items in the text:

- Key or repeated words and ideas
- Key themes
- Transition words (e.g., therefore, but, because, if/then, likewise, etc.)
- Lists
- Comparisons and contrasts
- Commands
- Unfamiliar words (look these up in a dictionary)
- Questions you have about the text

02 *Interpretation*
KEY QUESTION: WHAT DOES THE TEXT MEAN?

Once you have annotated the text, work through the following steps to help you interpret its meaning:

- Read the passage in other versions for a better understanding of the text.
- Read cross-references to help interpret Scripture with Scripture.
- Paraphrase or summarize the passage to check for understanding.
- Identify how the text reflects the metanarrative of Scripture, which is the story of creation, fall, redemption, and restoration.
- Read trustworthy commentaries if you need further insight into the meaning of the passage.

Application
KEY QUESTION: HOW SHOULD THE TRUTH OF THIS PASSAGE CHANGE ME?

Bible study is not merely an intellectual pursuit. The truths about God, ourselves, and the gospel that we discover in Scripture should produce transformation in our hearts and lives. Answer the following questions and prompts as you consider what you have learned in your study:

- What attributes of God's character are revealed in the passage?
- Consider places where the text directly states the character of God, as well as how His character is revealed through His words and actions.
- What do I learn about myself in light of who God is?
- Consider how you fall short of God's character, how the text reveals your sin nature, and what it says about your new identity in Christ.
- How should this truth change me?
- A passage of Scripture may contain direct commands telling us what to do or warnings about sins to avoid in order to help us grow in holiness. Other times, our application flows out of seeing ourselves in light of God's character. As we pray and reflect on how God is calling us to change in light of His Word, we should be asking questions like, "How should I pray for God to change my heart?" and "What practical steps can I take toward cultivating habits of holiness?"

Timeline of Scripture

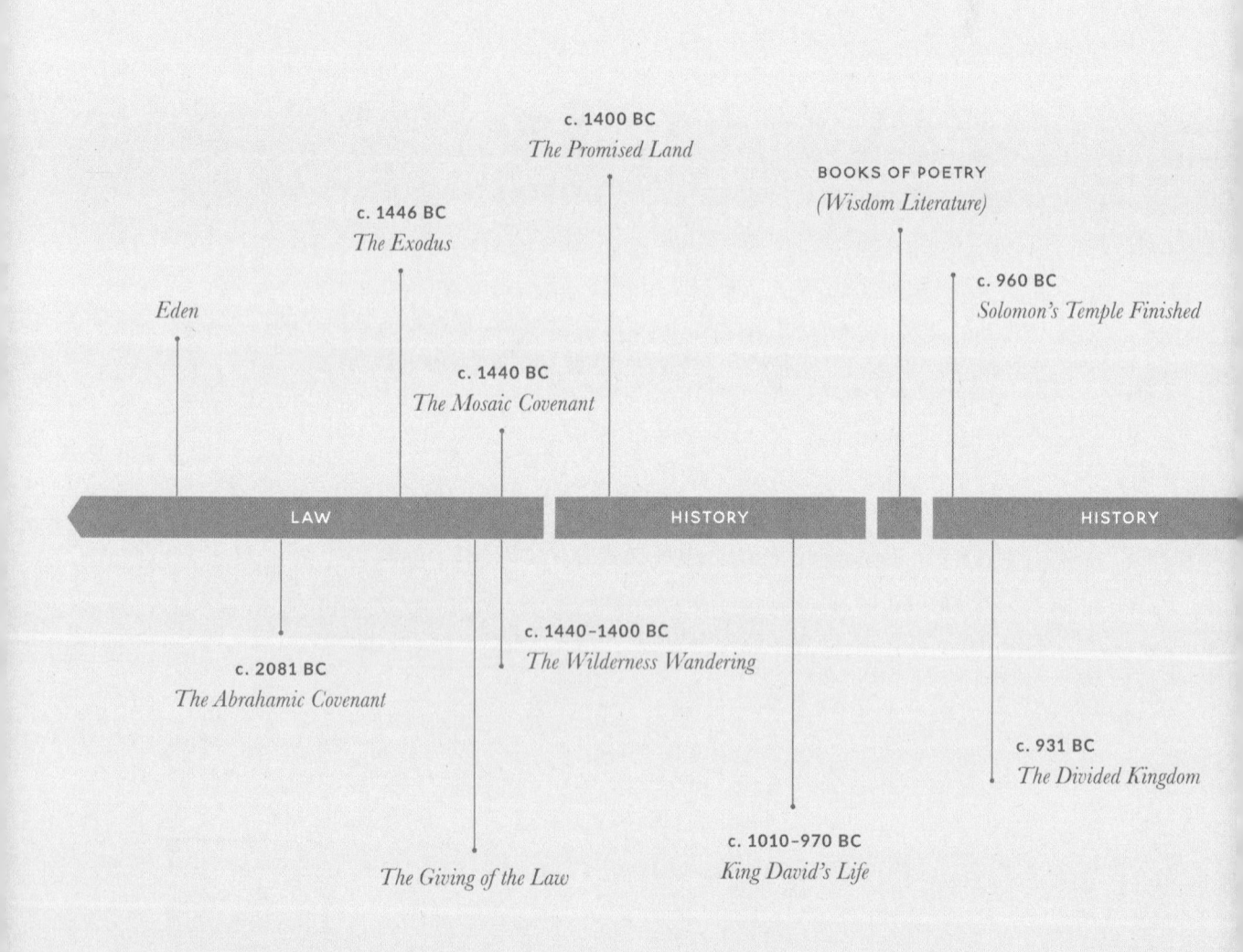

Eden

c. 2081 BC
The Abrahamic Covenant

c. 1446 BC
The Exodus

c. 1440 BC
The Mosaic Covenant

The Giving of the Law

c. 1440–1400 BC
The Wilderness Wandering

c. 1400 BC
The Promised Land

c. 1010–970 BC
King David's Life

BOOKS OF POETRY
(Wisdom Literature)

c. 960 BC
Solomon's Temple Finished

c. 931 BC
The Divided Kingdom

LAW | HISTORY | HISTORY

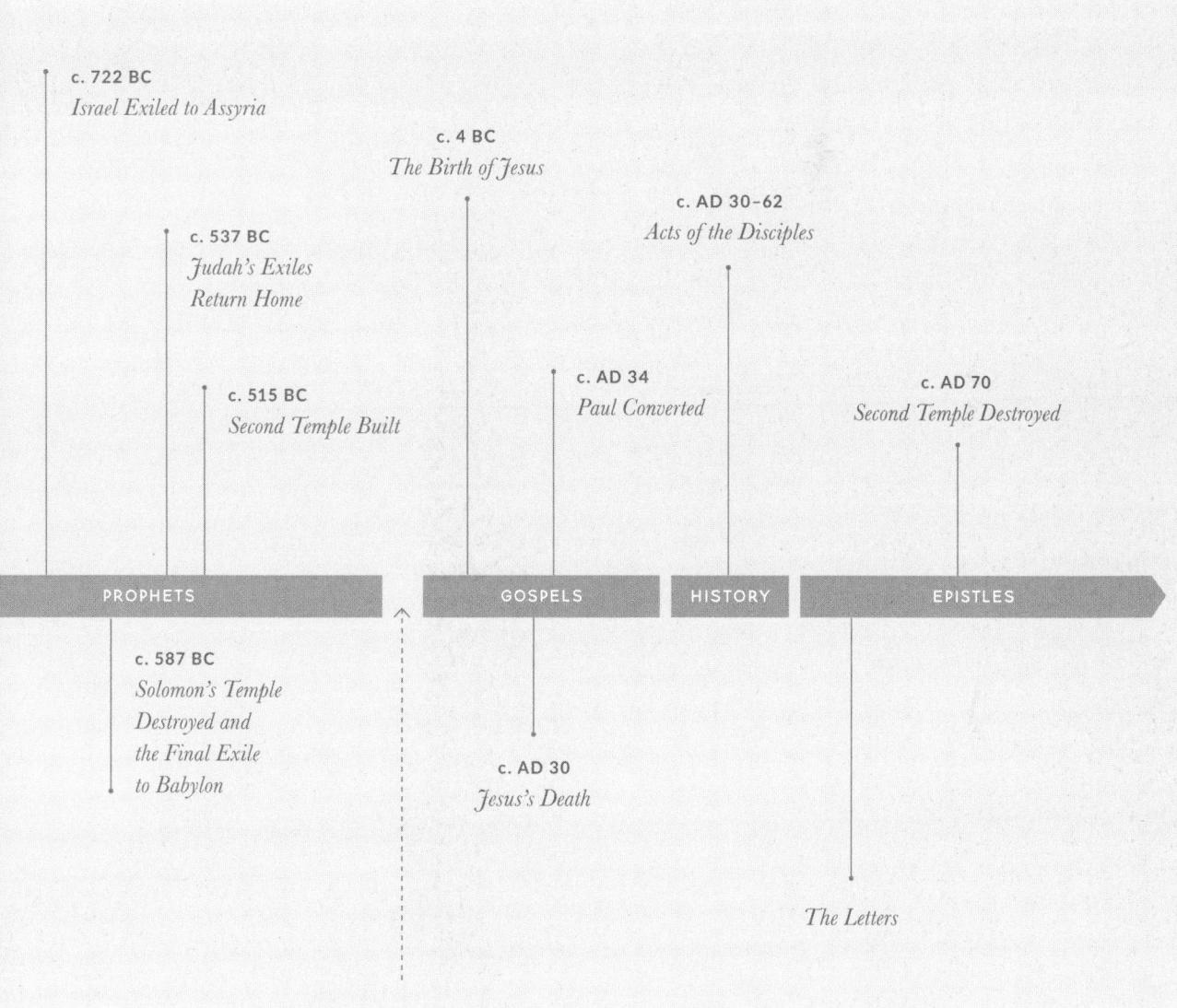

c. 722 BC
Israel Exiled to Assyria

c. 537 BC
Judah's Exiles Return Home

c. 4 BC
The Birth of Jesus

c. AD 30-62
Acts of the Disciples

c. 515 BC
Second Temple Built

c. AD 34
Paul Converted

c. AD 70
Second Temple Destroyed

| PROPHETS | GOSPELS | HISTORY | EPISTLES |

c. 587 BC
Solomon's Temple Destroyed and the Final Exile to Babylon

c. AD 30
Jesus's Death

The Letters

The Intertestamental Period

Timeline of Scripture / 17

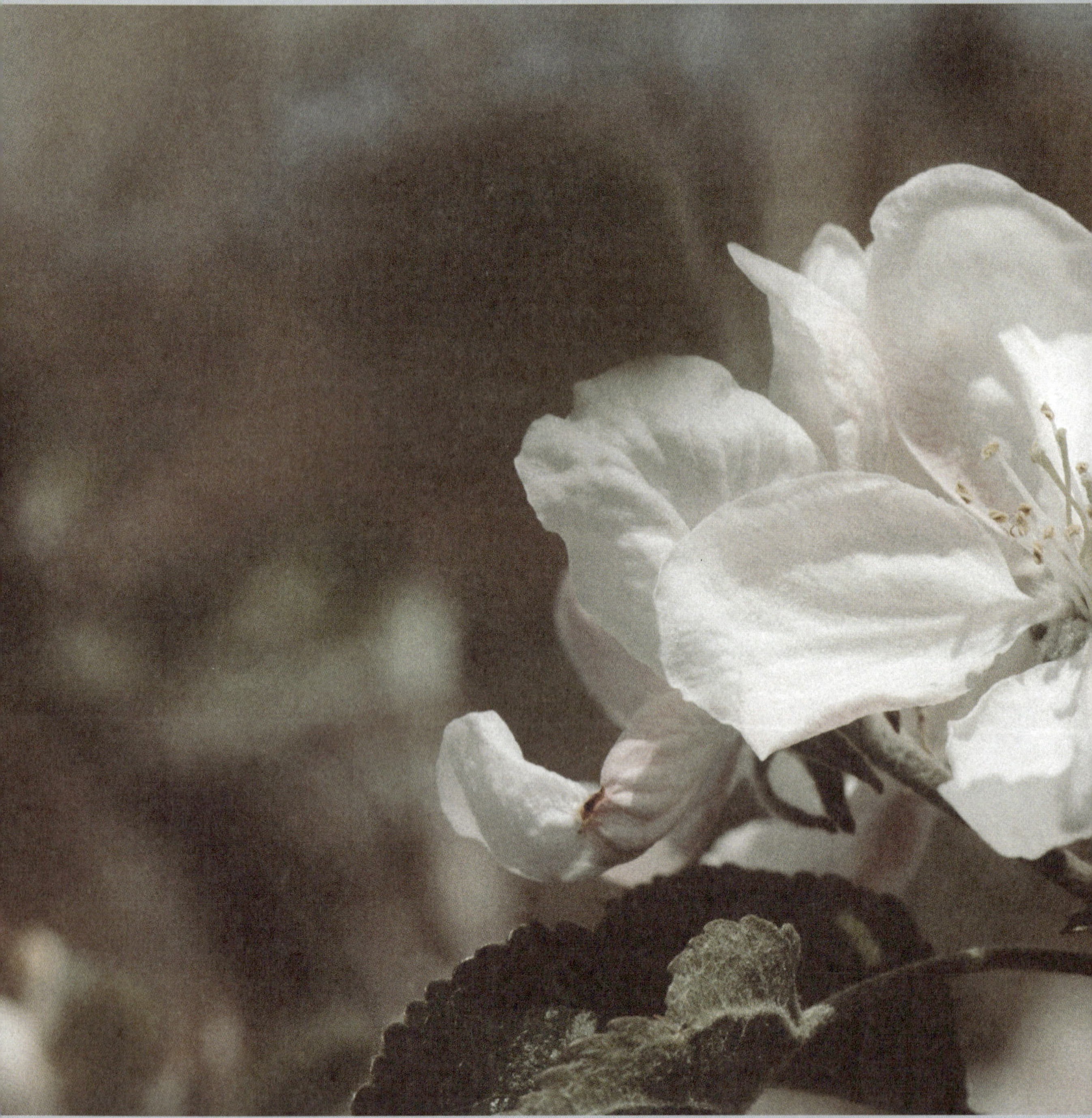

WEEK 27

Introduction

This week, you will read Ezra 3:10–11 and Ephesians 2:11–22. In looking at these passages, you will learn how believers are the new temple with Jesus Christ as their Cornerstone. In response to this great truth, you will be encouraged to glorify the Lord and point others to Him through the unity you share with fellow believers.

Mark it Up: Old Testament Passage

Today, we will begin our study of Ezra 3:10–11, a passage that describes how the Israelites began rebuilding the temple after they returned from being exiled. Read the passage two or three times and annotate, or mark up, the text as you read. For tips and examples on annotating, see pages 204–215.

Highlight any words or phrases that point to Christ.

Make note of any attributes of God seen in the text.

Circle every mention of the word "praise."

How do the people show their praise, according to this passage?

Underline the song of thanksgiving in verse 11.
Why are the people praising the Lord?

EZRA 3:10-11

¹⁰ When the builders had laid the foundation of the Lord's temple, the priests,

dressed in their robes and holding trumpets, and the Levites descended from Asaph,

holding cymbals, took their positions to praise the Lord, as King David of Israel had

instructed. ¹¹ They sang with praise and thanksgiving to the Lord: "For he is good;

his faithful love to Israel endures forever." Then all the people gave a great shout

of praise to the Lord because the foundation of the Lord's house had been laid.

Go Deeper

> Read Ezra 3:10–11.

Imagine that you are a little kid playing with some building blocks. You have spent hours meticulously placing your blocks together, forming the blocks into a big house. After placing the final block on the top, you step back to admire your work with joy. But suddenly, your sibling comes into the room and crashes into your building. All of the blocks come tumbling to the ground, and your perfect creation is ruined.

The Israelites experienced something similar with the temple. The temple was a glorious place in the midst of Jerusalem. It was where God's presence dwelled and was a sign of God's covenant, the promise that He was with His people. The temple was a gift of God's grace, as the people had the opportunity to draw near to the Lord and have their sins atoned for through sacrifice. As long as the people remained obedient to the Lord, the temple would remain, and God's presence would stay. But this beautiful house and the gift of God's presence would be ruined if the people disobeyed.

> Read 1 Kings 9:6–9. What would happen to the temple, according to these verses? Why would this happen?

_____

_____

_____

_____

_____

_____

Sadly, the warning God gave to Solomon in 1 Kings 9:6–9 came true, and the temple was destroyed during the Babylonian siege (2 Kings 25:8–15). Not only was the temple destroyed, but the Israelites were taken captive and exiled from their land. However, in His infinite mercy and faithfulness, God restored His people, making a way for a remnant of the Israelites to come back to their land and begin again. Ezra 3:10–11 takes place after this remnant has been brought back due to King Cyrus's proclamation allowing Israel to return and rebuild the temple.

> Read Ezra 1:1–4. How do you see God's sovereignty and faithfulness at work in this passage?

The rebuilding of the temple is incredibly significant for Israel. It symbolizes God's presence with His people again—that He is still with them, faithfully fulfilling His promises to them. Rebuilding the temple also symbolizes the rebuilding of God's people. God promised Israel restoration even though they had sinned (Jeremiah 29:10–14), and now that the Israelites have returned, they are not only restored to their land but also restored to their God. In light of God's restoration, grace, and faithfulness, Israel has the chance to respond with repentance and renewed obedience to the Lord.

Although only the temple foundation has been laid, the people respond with shouts of praise and declarations of God's faithfulness. Such a celebration echoes the celebration that occurred when the temple was first built (2 Chronicles 5:13). God has been faithful, and because of His faithfulness, Israel can rejoice and have hope. For as the temple is being built up, the Israelites are being built up in the process into a people shaped for God's glory.

> How can you praise the Lord for the ways He has been faithful in your life? Pray a prayer of praise to Him now, thanking Him for what He has done for you.

Jesus Himself builds believers
"into a holy temple in the Lord."

W27 / D3

Mark it Up: New Testament Passage

Now that we have studied the rebuilding of the temple in Ezra 3:10–11, we will turn to the New Testament to see how Jesus Himself builds believers "into a holy temple in the Lord" (Ephesians 2:21). Read Ephesians 2:11–22 two or three times and annotate, or mark up, the text as you read. For tips and examples on annotating, see pages 204–215.

Highlight any words or phrases that point to Christ.

Make note of any attributes of God seen in the text.

Circle the phrase "but now" in verse 13.
What has Jesus done for the Gentiles, according to this verse?

Underline every mention of the word "one."

According to verse 19, who were the Gentiles before, and who are they now in Christ?

Circle how Jesus is described in verse 20.

What do verses 21–22 say is happening to God's people?

Week 27 Day 3 • Mark it Up: New Testament Passage / 25

EPHESIANS 2:11–22

¹¹ So, then, remember that at one time you were Gentiles in the flesh—called "the uncircumcised" by those called "the circumcised," which is done in the flesh by human hands. ¹² At that time you were without Christ, excluded from the citizenship of Israel, and foreigners to the covenants of promise, without hope and without God in the world. ¹³ But now in Christ Jesus, you who were far away have been brought near by the blood of Christ. ¹⁴ For he is our peace, who made both groups one and tore down the dividing wall of hostility. In his flesh, ¹⁵ he made of no effect the law consisting of commands and expressed in regulations, so that he might create in himself one new man from the two,

resulting in peace. ¹⁶ He did this so that he might reconcile both to God in one body through the cross by which he put the hostility to death. ¹⁷ He came and proclaimed the good news of peace to you who were far away and peace to those who were near. ¹⁸ For through him we both have access in one Spirit to the Father.

¹⁹ So, then, you are no longer foreigners and strangers, but fellow citizens with the saints, and members of God's household, ²⁰ built on the foundation of the apostles and prophets, with Christ Jesus himself as the cornerstone. ²¹ In him the whole building, being put together, grows into a holy temple in the Lord.

²² In him you are also being built together for God's dwelling in the Spirit.

Make the Christ Connection

> Read Ezra 3:10–11 and Ephesians 2:11–22.

For many years, the Gentiles, or non-Jewish people, were separated from God's people, the Jews. This separation began back in Genesis 15, when God made a covenant with Abraham, the father of the Jewish nation. God promised Abraham that He would make him into a great nation by blessing him with descendants as numerous as the stars (Genesis 15:5). And God confirmed this promise with Abraham's descendants—patriarchs like Isaac, Jacob, and David—thus forming Abraham's descendants into His covenant people.

Initially, this covenant did not include those from outside of Abraham's family tree—and so, throughout the generations, there was separation between the Jews and the Gentiles and often hostility. But it was God's plan from the very beginning for people from all nations to be part of His family (Ephesians 1:4–5, 11; Galatians 3:8). Although He first formed His covenant with Abraham and his descendants, God's plan and desire was to do something new through Christ by reconciling both Jews and Gentiles to Himself. Now, because of Jesus's sacrifice, anyone who places their faith in Him is brought into God's household.

> Read Galatians 3:27–28 and John 10:14–16. What do these passages teach us about God's people? How are we to live as believers because of the unity we have as brothers and sisters in Christ?

Christ's salvation unites both Jew and Gentile, making them one people, one household for God's glory. But this is no ordinary household. As God's people with God's presence living inside of us through the Spirit, we are considered the new temple (1 Corinthians 6:19–20). No longer do we have to go to a physical temple to worship God and draw near to Him. Because of Jesus's sacrifice, the veil has been torn (Matthew 27:51), and we are no longer separated from God; we are able to worship the Lord wherever we go. And with the Holy Spirit inside of us, we are able to draw near to the Lord always. As the new temple, we are meant to display God's glory, just as the temple in the Old Testament was meant to display God's glory.

> Read 1 Peter 2:4–5. How does Peter describe believers in this passage? How is this connected to what Paul teaches in Ephesians 2:11–22?

Just like the temple and the Israelites were being rebuilt in Ezra, so are all believers being "rebuilt" through Christ. We were once separated from God and living in our sin, but Christ's salvation has made us new, and we are restored in our relationship with God. Through Christ and by the Spirit, we are being built up as a people to be a spiritual house that worships and glorifies the Lord. It is Jesus who is the Cornerstone of this spiritual house, meaning that it is because of Him that we are able to be this renewed and restored people for God's own glory. We are united because Christ is the One who unites us. Just as a cornerstone keeps a house together, so Christ keeps us together by His grace.

Because Jesus is our Cornerstone, we are secure in Him. As we depend on Christ's power and follow Him, we will continue to grow in our Christlikeness. We will continue to be built up as a people who point others to God's greatness and the hope of the gospel, inviting all people to come and be part of God's household.

> Thank Jesus for the relationship you have with God and the unity you have with other believers through Him who is your Cornerstone.

Live it Out

Read Ezra 3:10–11 and Ephesians 2:11–22.

Jesus is our Cornerstone, and He is building us as believers into a house for God's glory. As the new temple, we are promised that Jesus is holding us together, motivating us to depend on Christ in all circumstances. We are promised that God is with us wherever we go, encouraging us to rest in His presence that is with us. Not only this, but we are also privileged to point others to Jesus. The glory of the temple and the worship of God's people was like a light that beckoned the nations to come near. Living faithfully and obediently as believers, through the help of the Spirit, will cause us to shine brightly in this broken world, inviting others to come to know the God we serve (Philippians 2:15–16, Matthew 5:16).

For us to live faithfully and obediently as believers, we must live out the unity that is ours in Christ. We must treat other believers as the brothers and sisters that they are by loving them and building one another up with encouragement (1 Thessalonians 5:11). We must also live out our purpose as believers by glorifying the Lord with our actions and proclaiming the gospel to those around us. Because maintaining unity and glorifying the Lord cannot be accomplished in our own power, we must rely on the Spirit, the One who is building us up through our sanctification (Ephesians 2:21–22).

As we rely on the Spirit to help us walk in unity and obedience, we can look forward to the day when our "building" will be complete. One day, Christ will return, our sanctification will be complete, and we will dwell fully in the presence of God forever (Revelation 21:3).

Reflect on this week's verses as you answer the following questions.

How can you practically seek unity with other brothers and sisters in Christ?

Read 1 Corinthians 6:19–20. How can you glorify God with your body?

What does it look like to see and respond to Jesus as your Cornerstone in your daily life?

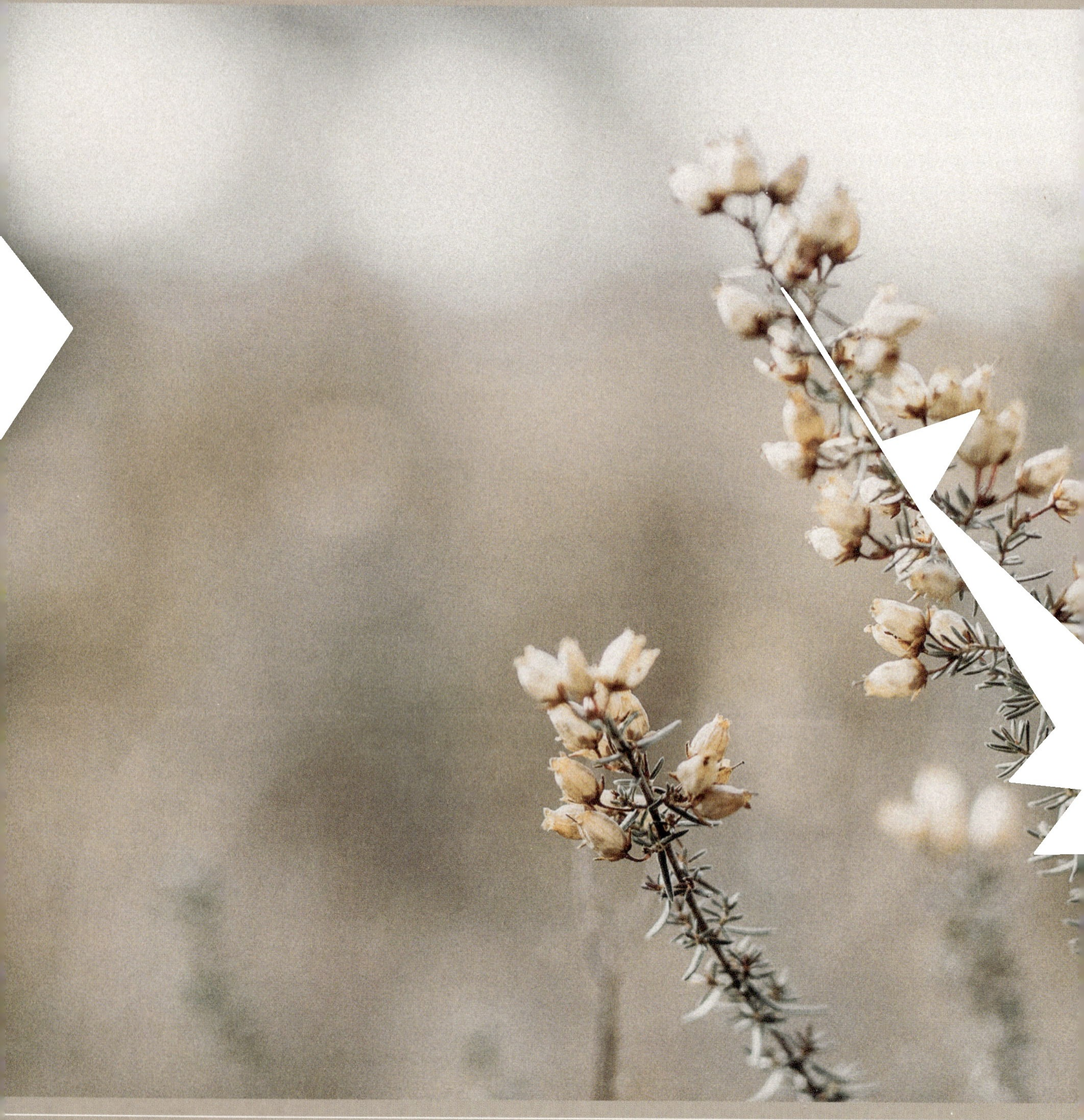

WEEK 28

Introduction

This week, we will trace the themes of suffering and obedience through Job 1:20–22 and Matthew 26:36–46, learning how Jesus is our obedient Servant who suffered for us on the cross. In response, you will be encouraged to obey the Lord and endure suffering by resting in Christ's presence and looking to eternity, where suffering will be no more.

Mark it Up: Old Testament Passage

Today, we will begin studying Job 1:20–22 as we learn of Job's faithfulness and steadfastness in the midst of deep suffering. Read the passage two or three times and annotate, or mark up, the text as you read. For tips and examples on annotating, see pages 204–215.

Highlight any words or phrases that point to Christ.

Make note of any attributes of God seen in the text.

The first chapter of Job describes the beginnings of Job's suffering. What is Job's response to this suffering in verse 20?

Underline what Job says the Lord does in verse 21.

What is Job's response to the Lord?
What do you think this tells us of Job's trust in God?

JOB 1:20–22

[20] Then Job stood up, tore his robe, and shaved his head.

He fell to the ground and worshiped, [21] saying:

Naked I came from my mother's womb,

and naked I will leave this life.

The Lord gives, and the Lord takes away.

Blessed be the name of the Lord.

[22] Throughout all this Job did not sin or blame God for anything.

Go Deeper

Read Job 1:20–22.

Each one of us encounters suffering, no matter how hard we might try to avoid it. Our world is desperately broken, causing every person to experience the consequences of the Fall through trials, troubles, and grievances. But why does God allow suffering? Many people find themselves wrestling with this difficult question in light of the brokenness of this world, but the Bible gives us truth that helps settle our confused minds and troubled hearts. In the book of Job specifically, we learn what it looks like to trust God in our suffering and see how God purposefully works through our suffering.

The book of Job tells the story of Job, a man who fears the Lord and is faithful to Him. One day, Satan approaches God and asks to test Job's faith. Satan wants to see if Job will remain obedient to the Lord after having everything taken from him. God permits Satan to test Job, and as a result, all of Job's children, servants, and possessions are wiped away. Job is left with nothing.

How would you respond if you experienced such a tragedy?

Job responds with expressions of grief and mourning by tearing his robe and shaving his head. But even though Job mourns, he also worships. He declares the truth that God has the ability to give and take away as He so pleases, and he blesses God's name. Job 1:22 also tells us that Job does not blame God or sin against God throughout this suffering.

As we go through the rest of the book of Job, we see Job's suffering increase. God allows Satan to afflict Job with boils all over his body. Yet when Job's wife tells him to curse the Lord and die, Job responds by saying, "Should we accept only good from God and not adversity?" (Job 2:10).

Even though he experiences miserable suffering, Job does not sin against the Lord. And when his friends give him questionable advice in the midst of his sorrow, Job continues to be obedient to God. Although Job does wrestle with the cause of his suffering, he never accuses God of being unfair. He never speaks lies about the Lord or makes unjust remarks about His character and ways. He never curses the Lord for allowing him to suffer in this way. Job understands that God has allowed Satan to bring affliction upon him (Job 1:12, 20–22; 2:4–6), yet Job seeks to trust and remain obedient to God through it all.

> Read Job 42:10–17. How does God restore Job?

God eventually speaks to Job from a whirlwind, humbling Job as He declares His great sovereignty (Job 38:1). While Job does not receive exact answers for why he has experienced suffering, he is able to humble himself before the Lord and trust that God's ways are always purposeful. And when God restores Job's fortunes, Job is able to see that even though suffering is painful, God still works through that suffering to redeem and restore.

> Praise the Lord for His ability and desire to bring about restoration from suffering.

Stay awake and pray,
so that you won't enter
into temptation.
The spirit is willing,
but the flesh is weak.

MATTHEW 26:41

W28 / D3

Mark it Up: New Testament Passage

Today, we shift from the Old Testament to the New Testament to learn about Jesus's perfect obedience in His suffering before He went to the cross. Read Matthew 26:36–46 two or three times and annotate, or mark up, the text as you read. For tips and examples on annotating, see pages 204–215.

Highlight any words or phrases that point to Christ.

Make note of any attributes of God seen in the text.

Circle the words that describe how Jesus is feeling in verses 37–38.

Underline Jesus's prayer to the Lord in verses 39 and 42.
What does Jesus ask from God?

Highlight in another color Jesus's words in verses 45–46.
According to these verses, what is about to happen to Him?

MATTHEW 26:36–46

³⁶ Then Jesus came with them to a place called Gethsemane, and he told the disciples, "Sit here while I go over there and pray." ³⁷ Taking along Peter and the two sons of Zebedee, he began to be sorrowful and troubled. ³⁸ He said to them, "I am deeply grieved to the point of death. Remain here and stay awake with me." ³⁹ Going a little farther, he fell facedown and prayed, "My Father, if it is possible, let this cup pass from me. Yet not as I will, but as you will."

⁴⁰ Then he came to the disciples and found them sleeping. He asked Peter, "So, couldn't you stay awake with me one hour? ⁴¹ Stay awake and pray, so that

you won't enter into temptation. The spirit is willing, but the flesh is weak."

[42] Again, a second time, he went away and prayed, "My Father, if this cannot pass unless I drink it, your will be done." [43] And he came again and found them sleeping, because they could not keep their eyes open. [44] After leaving them, he went away again and prayed a third time, saying the same thing once more. [45] Then he came to the disciples and said to them, "Are you still sleeping and resting? See, the time is near. The Son of Man is betrayed into the hands of sinners. [46] Get up; let's go. See, my betrayer is near."

Make the Christ Connection

Read Job 1:20–22 and Matthew 26:36–46.

Throughout His suffering, Job demonstrated the importance of remaining obedient and faithful to the Lord. But while Job was faithful to the Lord, he was still a sinner. Job was not perfect in his obedience to the Lord, but there is One who is completely blameless and faithful to the Lord—Jesus Christ. In Matthew 26:36–46, we see how Jesus remains obedient to the Lord, even in the face of death.

Throughout His ministry, Jesus knows that God's plan involves Him dying on the cross, and when it comes to the time of Passover, Jesus understands that He will soon experience this death. After eating a Passover meal with His disciples in Matthew 26:17–30, Jesus retreats to the garden of Gethsemane to pray. He takes Peter, James, and John with Him but goes away from them by Himself to pray to the Lord. It is in this place that Jesus prays a raw and honest prayer to God. Jesus knows the immense suffering He will experience on the cross, and He asks God to make another way, to take away the cup of wrath that will be poured out upon Him. But even though Jesus asks this of the Lord, He yields to God's plan. Jesus does not stray from God's will but embraces God's will, even though doing so will cost Him His life.

What does it say of Christ's obedience and endurance that He would accept God's will for Him to go to the cross?

Jesus's experience in the garden of Gethsemane demonstrates complete obedience in a time of utter grief and pain. Such an experience reflects Job's story, as Jesus, too, remains faithful to the Father. But although Job suffered, Jesus goes on to suffer far more greatly. Jesus is mocked and beaten, and He is nailed to the cross, where He drinks the cup of suffering on our behalf and offers Himself as a sacrifice for our sins. Like Job, Jesus's friends are of no comfort to Him. One betrays Him. One denies Him. Only one remains by His side (John 19:25–26). Yet, though alone, Jesus endures to the end. He willingly gives up His life on the cross, taking on the full burden of our sin and shame.

> Read Matthew 27:28–29 and Isaiah 53:3–12.
> How does Jesus's suffering impact or humble you?

_____

But God's plan does not end with Jesus's death. Three days after Jesus is laid in the tomb, God raises Jesus from the grave. Just as God restored Job's fortunes on the other side of his suffering, so does God restore Jesus's life. And because of Christ's utter obedience, God has given Him the name that is above every name (Philippians 2:8–9). The gospel reminds us of the lengths Jesus went to for our salvation and boasts of the truth that on the other side of suffering is glory.

> Thank Jesus for the suffering He experienced as He went to the cross for you. Praise God for working through Jesus's suffering to bring about restoration and salvation.

Live it Out

Read Job 1:20–22 and Matthew 26:36–46.

Jesus is our suffering Servant who chose to die so that we could be saved. But even though Jesus took on our punishment upon the cross, being a follower of Christ does not mean we will live a life devoid of suffering. In fact, the Christian life is a life of suffering (John 16:33), as we live in a broken world full of people who oppose God and His kingdom. But Jesus is worth the suffering we experience. Though our circumstances may be unpleasant, we have hope in our suffering, as God uses our suffering to shape our faith and grow us in our Christlikeness (Romans 5:3–5). And we have hope for our suffering, for we know we have an eternal home free from suffering that awaits us.

When we, like Job, find ourselves struggling under the weight of our suffering, we can remember the endurance of our Savior. We can remember Jesus's complete obedience and perseverance in the face of death. Christ's obedience and endurance motivates our own, reminding us that through the power of the Spirit, we can remain faithful to the Lord and endure any hardship in our lives. In our trials, we can be reminded that Jesus sympathizes with our sufferings (Hebrews 4:15).

Jesus suffered alone so that we would never have to. We can be comforted and encouraged by Christ's presence with us through the trials we face. As we rely on His presence with us and rest in the power of the Spirit, we will be able to endure every trial, knowing that one day, all suffering will end and we will dwell with God forever.

Reflect on this week's verses as you answer the following questions.

How do you usually respond during times of suffering?

_____
_____
_____
_____
_____
_____

What would it look like to be faithful to the Lord, even in your suffering?

Read 1 Peter 5:10 and Romans 8:18. How do these verses encourage you?

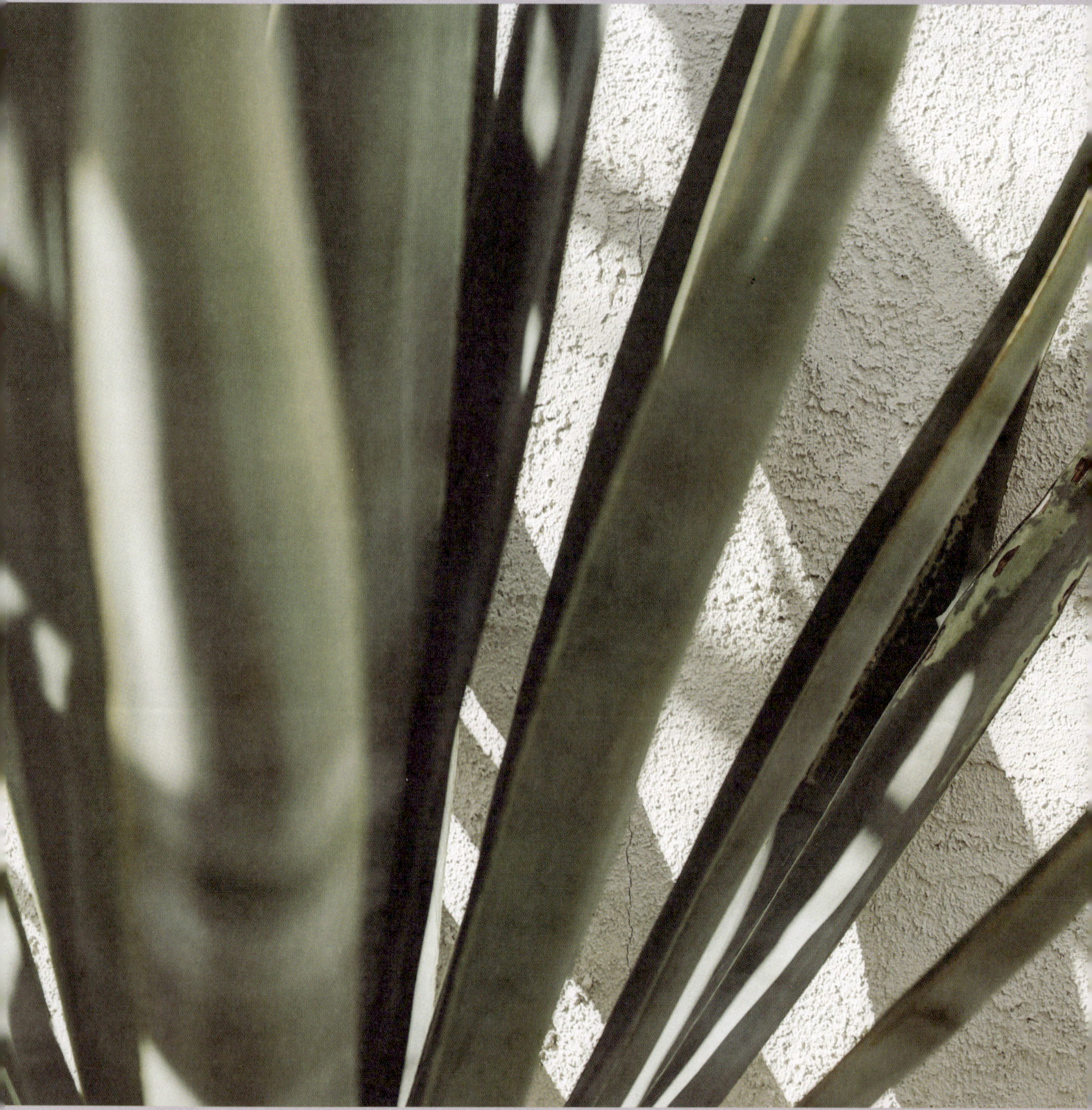

WEEK 29

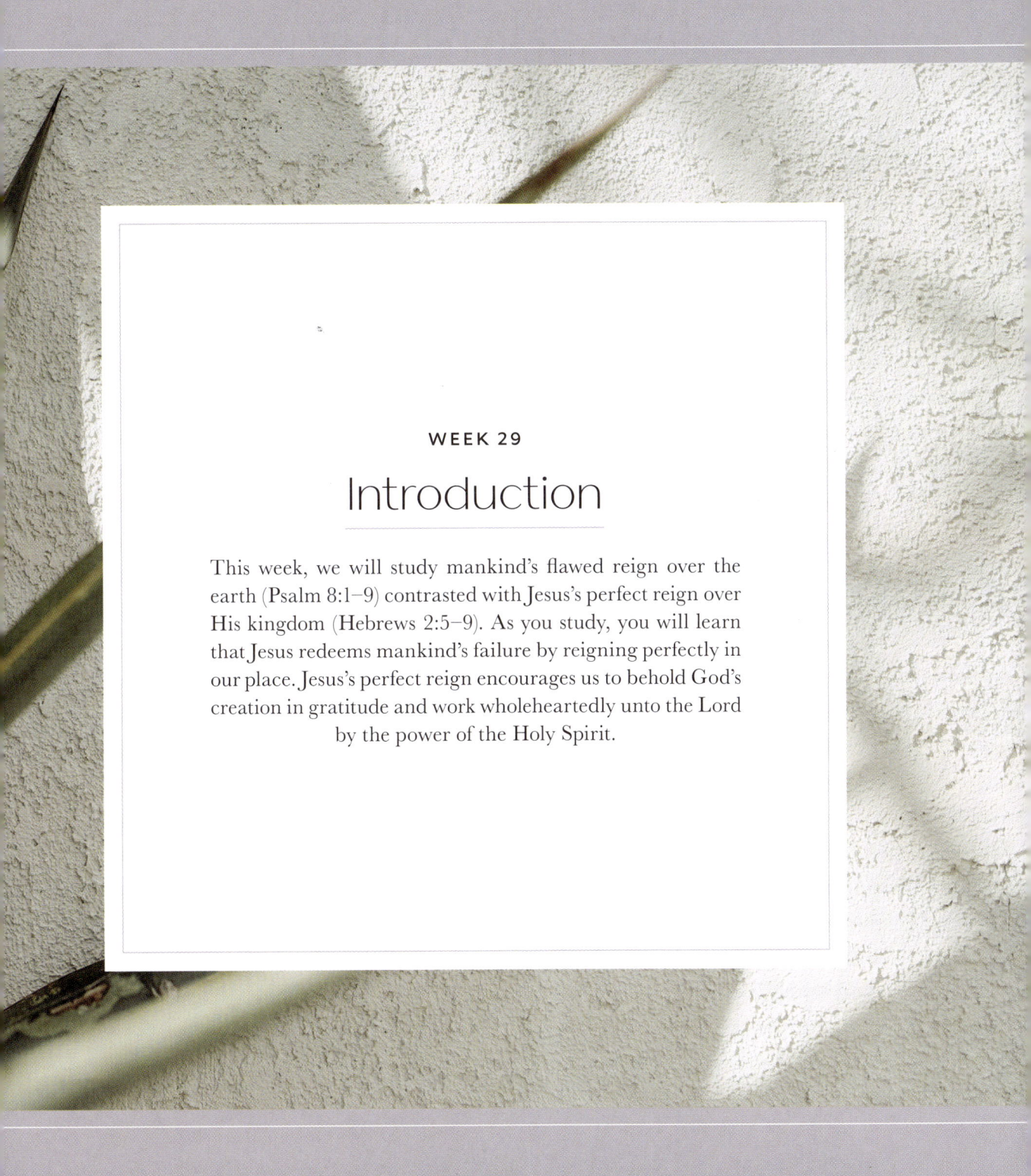

Introduction

This week, we will study mankind's flawed reign over the earth (Psalm 8:1–9) contrasted with Jesus's perfect reign over His kingdom (Hebrews 2:5–9). As you study, you will learn that Jesus redeems mankind's failure by reigning perfectly in our place. Jesus's perfect reign encourages us to behold God's creation in gratitude and work wholeheartedly unto the Lord by the power of the Holy Spirit.

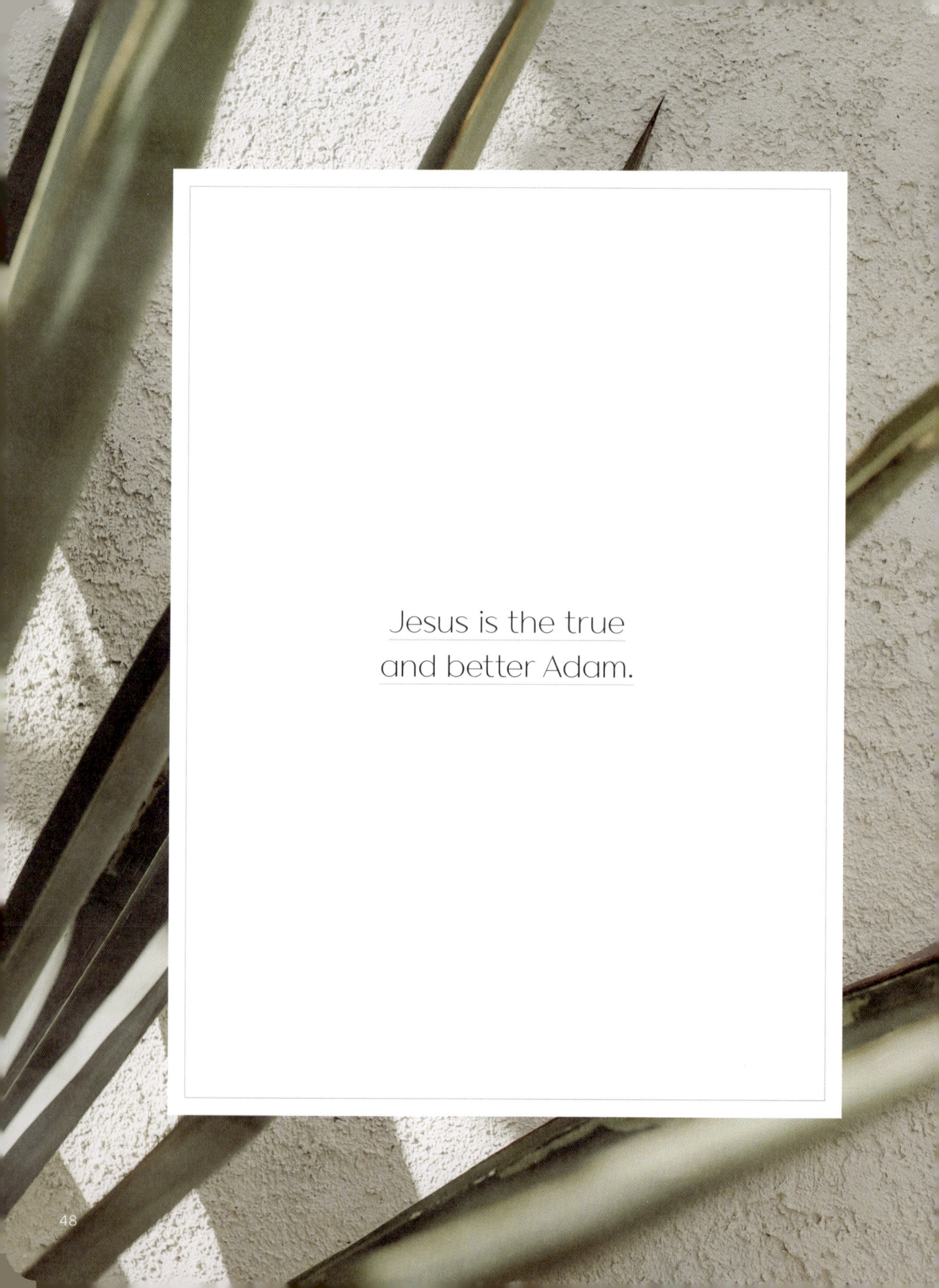

Jesus is the true
and better Adam.

Mark it Up: Old Testament Passage

Today, we will begin studying Psalm 8:1–9. This psalm of David will prepare us to contrast mankind's flawed reign over creation with Christ's perfect reign later in the week, ultimately showing us that Jesus is the true and better Adam. Read the passage two or three times and annotate, or mark up, the text as you read. For tips and examples on annotating, see pages 204–215.

> Highlight any words or phrases that point to Christ.

> Make note of any attributes of God seen in the text.

> Underline anything in these verses that God has created.

> Verses 5–6 share how God has honored mankind. Circle how God does so in these verses. How has God elevated mankind above the rest of His creation?

> Highlight the first and last verse in this psalm.
> How does this repetition fuel your worship of God?

PSALM 8:1–9

¹ Lord, our Lord,

how magnificent is your name throughout the earth!

You have covered the heavens with your majesty.

² From the mouths of infants and nursing babies,

you have established a stronghold

on account of your adversaries

in order to silence the enemy and the avenger.

³ When I observe your heavens,

the work of your fingers,

the moon and the stars,

which you set in place,

⁴ what is a human being that you remember him,

a son of man that you look after him?

⁵ You made him little less than God

and crowned him with glory and honor.

⁶ You made him ruler over the works of your hands;

you put everything under his feet:

⁷ all the sheep and oxen,

as well as the animals in the wild,

⁸ the birds of the sky,

and the fish of the sea

that pass through the currents of the seas.

⁹ Lord, our Lord,

how magnificent is your name throughout the earth!

Go Deeper

Read Psalm 8:1–9.

As David meditates upon the majesty of God's creation, he is overcome with worship. David reflects upon the vastness of the moon and the stars—all created by the fingers of God—as if the whole universe could fit in the palm of His hand. And this leads David to awe. If God could create a planet with His fingers, what is mankind that He is mindful of them? How can such a mighty God care so tenderly for lowly mankind?

Read Genesis 1:26–28. In whose image did God craft mankind?

God crowned mankind with glory and honor by creating them in His own image. He gave them the ability to think, create, and care for His creation, and they were to be image-bearers, shining a light of God's goodness across the world. But mankind failed to be the caretakers God created them to be. They doubted God's good instruction and lifted their own desires above their love for God. When Adam and Eve ate the forbidden fruit, sin and sin's consequences flooded into the world. Reigning over God's creation now seemed less like a privilege and more like a burden.

Read Genesis 3:16–24. What were the consequences of sin for mankind?

Even in their sin, God did not revoke Adam and Eve's identity as image-bearers. Instead, their disordered desires would struggle against a creation ordered to magnify God. Their lives would be scarred by pain, selfishness, exhaustion, and weariness. The ground would grow thorns and thistles, frustrating mankind's hard work. Labor would fill mankind with groans instead of joy. And yet, even now, man continually chooses himself above God—disgracing their God-given dignity—by participating in sin.

And man does not only reign over the fields and the animals; mankind also exercises dominion over one another in the form of rulers and kings. But even this has been tarnished by sin. God was to be the King of His creation. He ruled perfectly, protecting and caring for His people. And yet, by choosing sin, His people rejected His kingship—desiring to rule themselves in their own strength. They desired an earthly king to rule over them, and God graciously fulfilled this request in 1 Samuel 8.

> Even before the Israelites entered the Promised Land, God knew they would ask for a king, so He communicated this future king's responsibility in Deuteronomy 17:14–17. According to this passage, what were the king's responsibilities to be?

This king was to rule Israel in the way of the Lord, but as you can likely guess, the Israelite kings failed over and over again to reign in the way God commanded. They accumulated wealth for themselves, practiced polygamy, and held alliances with Egypt (1 Kings 3:1–3, 2 Kings 18:19–21). Though some kings were better than others, all were marred by sin. All squandered the good gift of dominion that God gave to mankind. All left the Israelites longing for the Promised Savior who would be their wonderful Counselor and Mighty God (Isaiah 9:6)—who would inherit the nations and possess the earth (Psalm 2:8).

The human race needed someone to reign in their place, someone who would lower Himself below the angels to redeem God's people. Humanity needed a King of glory and honor who would humble Himself as a Servant—a King born in a lowly manger.

Mark it Up: New Testament Passage

Today, we will read Hebrews 2:5–9 and observe Jesus's flawless reign over His kingdom—a reign marked by obedience to His Father in heaven. Read the passage multiple times and annotate, or mark up, the text as you read. For tips and examples on annotating, see pages 204–215.

Highlight any words or phrases that point to Christ.

Make note of any attributes of God seen in the text.

Open your Bible to Psalm 8. Highlight any language in Hebrews 2:5–9 that reflects language that you see in Psalm 8. How does this help us understand how Psalm 8 points to Christ?

Take a look at Hebrews 2:9 and circle any reference to Jesus's humility.

Draw a box around any conjunctions—words such as *for, and, nor, but, or, yet, so*—used in Hebrews 2:9. How does Jesus's glory and honor relate to His humility? What is the purpose of His death?

HEBREWS 2:5–9

⁵ For he has not subjected to angels the world to come that we

are talking about. ⁶ But someone somewhere has testified:

What is man that you remember him,

or the son of man that you care for him?

⁷ You made him lower than the angels

for a short time;

you crowned him with glory and honor

⁸ and subjected everything under his feet.

For in subjecting everything to him, he left nothing that is not subject to him.

As it is, we do not yet see everything subjected to him. ⁹ But we do see Jesus—

made lower than the angels for a short time so that by God's grace he might taste

death for everyone—crowned with glory and honor because he suffered death.

Make the Christ Connection

> Read Psalm 8 and Hebrews 2:5–9.

In Psalm 8, David reflected upon God's goodness and mercy to elevate humans as a "little less than God" (Psalm 8:5). God made mankind in His image—able to share love, to create, and to commune with God. Though human beings rebelled against God in sin and took God's love in vain, God never removed His image from them. The mercy of God brought David to worship.

Fast forward to the New Testament book of Hebrews. The author of Hebrews reflects upon Jesus as the pioneer of our faith—the One who tasted death in order to bring many sons and daughters to glory. To illustrate the humility of Christ, the author quotes Psalm 8:4–6. While God dignified humans by making them a "little less than God," Jesus temporarily forsook His dignity and home in heaven and humbled Himself by taking on the form of a human.

Jesus worked heartily for the Lord, accomplishing what we could never accomplish—perfect obedience to the Father. For the joy set before Him, Jesus endured the cross (Hebrews 12:2) so that God's people could be redeemed—as image-bearers in the family of God as they were meant to be all along. Jesus is the King crowned in glory and honor because of His humility and faithfulness to suffer death. Jesus reigns perfectly in mankind's place.

> Read Philippians 2:5–11. How does Jesus's humility contrast with mankind's desire to rule themselves, as we discussed in Day 2?

Jesus is not a King of extravagance who demands worship for fame and fortune. Jesus, though equal to God Himself, did not consider equality with God something to be grasped. Instead, He emptied Himself and took on the form of a servant in the likeness of humanity. The King of kings reigned in service of His kingdom. He humbled Himself by becoming obedient, even to death on a cross (Philippians 2:8).

> Read Romans 5:15–19. How does Jesus redeem mankind?

Jesus's obedience highly contrasts the disobedience of mankind, ushered forth from Adam and Eve's first bite of the forbidden fruit. Just as through one man's sin many were made sinners, so too through one man's obedience, many are redeemed and counted righteous.

While mankind disgraced their dignity as image-bearers, Jesus restores that same dignity. Death was given to all through Adam, but life is given through Christ. Jesus gives God's people righteousness, not because they earn it but because through their redemption, God is glorified.

> Read Hebrews 2:5–9 again.

While humanity sought after independence, Jesus came to reign in perfect dependence—submitting Himself below the angels, even to the point of death, to glorify His Father (Hebrews 2:7–9). Jesus was obedient and never wavered in worship.

This dependence on and obedience to the Lord is the hallmark of the King of kings and how mankind was meant to exercise dominion all along—in dependence and obedience to God alone.

Jesus is the last Adam (1 Corinthians 15:45–47), a giver of life by the Spirit. Jesus, who is God, made Himself lower than God, submitted Himself to God's will, and is now crowned in honor and glory. Jesus is the true and better King, leading His people in worship of the Father as He reigns in perfect glory, majesty, power, and authority before all time—now and forever (Jude 1:25).

Live it Out

> Read Psalm 8 and Hebrews 2:5–9.

This week, we have studied David's worship of God as Creator and God's choice to give humanity dominion over His creation. However, sin kept God's people from exercising this dominion in dependence and obedience. Mankind's dominion was meant to be worship, but it became quite the opposite—people took God's good gifts in vain.

But there would be a Ruler to come who would rule in wholehearted worship of His Father—King Jesus. When Jesus—our King of kings—came to earth, He was made a little lower than the angels for a short while and was obedient to His Father as He died upon the cross (Hebrews 2:7–9). Because of His perfect obedience, we look forward to a day when Christ will return, rid the world of sin, and put His enemy—Satan—under His feet forever. When Christ comes to earth, He will have full dominion over the new creation and will reign in honor and glory and praise forever (Revelation 5:9–14). This truth gives us hope as we face darkness in the world.

But not only does Jesus give us hope as He reigns as the King of kings; He empowers us to redeem our reign over God's creation. We read in Day 2 that while, in the beginning, God created man to be caretakers of His good creation, sin's consequences caused brokenness to enter the world, fracturing that reign. But eventually, Jesus would come to make a way for man's reign over creation to be restored, partially now and fully when He comes again. Until that day, He redeems our failure as He reigns perfectly in our place, and by grace through faith in Him, we are given power through the Holy Spirit, who allows us to model our lives after His own. We give thanks to God as we behold His creation and dedicate our lives—our work and all that we do—wholeheartedly to Him.

Reflect on this week's verses as you answer the following questions.

> How have these passages encouraged you this week?

> God has given each of us lives to steward for His glory.
> How can you better steward your life for His glory today?

> How does Christ's future reign over all of creation give you hope?

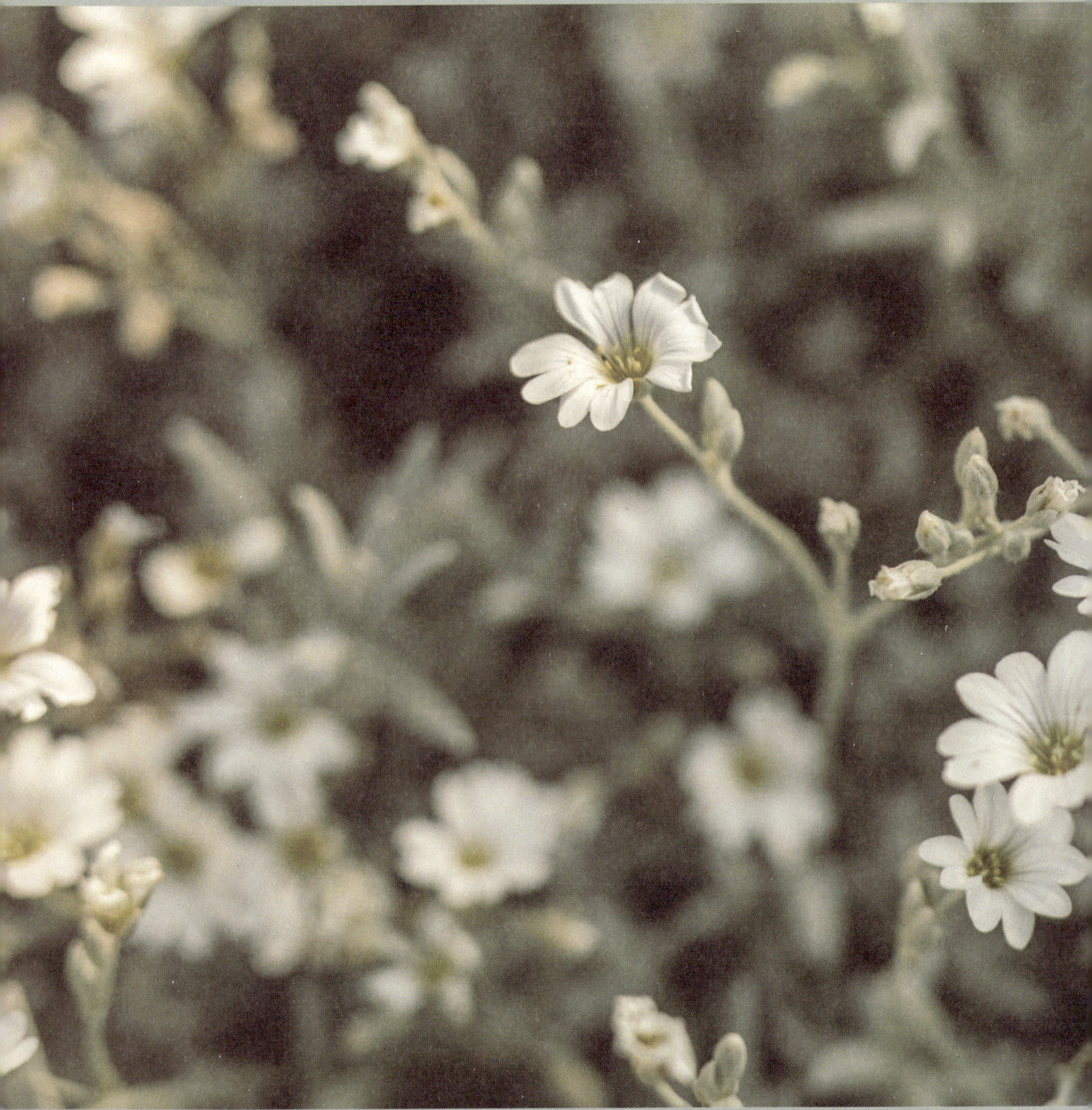

WEEK 30

Introduction

This week, we will look at Psalm 22, a psalm of anguish written by David and one that was quoted by Jesus as He hung on the cross in Matthew 27:45–50. We will consider how Jesus, too, experienced the despair found in this psalm, and we will be encouraged to voice and entrust our own pain to God, knowing He will come to our aid.

Mark it Up: Old Testament Passage

Today, we will begin studying Psalm 22:1–2. As we do, we will see how it was a fitting psalm for Jesus to quote on the cross, not just because of the pain represented in it but also because of how the psalm as a whole ends on a note of triumph. Read the passage multiple times and annotate, or mark up, the text as you read. For tips and examples on annotating, see pages 204–215.

Highlight any words or phrases that point to Christ.

Make note of any attributes of God seen in the text.

Circle words or phrases you see repeated.

Underline any words in the passage that may point to how David is feeling as he writes this psalm. How would you describe David's emotions in these two verses?

What does God's response to David seem to be?

PSALM 22:1–2

[1] My God, my God, why have you abandoned me?

Why are you so far from my deliverance

and from my words of groaning?

[2] My God, I cry by day, but you do not answer,

by night, yet I have no rest.

Go Deeper

> Read Psalm 22:1–31.

In his commentary on the Psalms, John Calvin wrote that he liked to call the book of Psalms "An Anatomy of all the Parts of the Soul," because "there is not an emotion of which any one can be conscious that is not here represented as in a mirror." That is, the highs and lows of life—and everything in between—are represented in its pages.

While many of David's psalms show us the highs of life, Psalm 22 shows us life's lows. We do not know when David wrote this psalm or what particular suffering he is responding to, but there is certainly no shortage of options. It could have been penned when he was a fugitive on the run from murderous King Saul (1 Samuel 19–30) or when he was being hunted by his own son Absalom years later (2 Samuel 15–17). Or it could have been another situation entirely. But to Calvin's point, part of the beauty of the Psalms is that we do not *need* to know David's specific circumstances. Rather, the psalms invite us to make their words our own when the feelings described in them match our own.

> Do you ever feel like you have been abandoned by God or that your prayers are not reaching Him?

In the case of Psalm 22, David expresses some strong emotions. He feels abandoned by God and as though God is not answering his prayers (verses 1–2). He sees himself as a "worm" that is scorned and despised by others (verses 6–7). That these people are "bulls" suggests that David is contending against some very strong adversaries (verse 12)—adversaries who mock his relationship with God, saying, "If the Lord loves [David] so much, let the Lord rescue him" (verse 8, NLT). David's heart melts. His strength is gone. He is surrounded by those who want to harm him. He feels alone (verses 11–18).

> In the midst of David's strong emotions, what does he remember about and ask of God? (See verses 3–5, 9–11, 19–21.)

While Psalm 22:1–21 is bleak, there are glimmers of hope. David recalls God's past faithfulness to him and to the Israelites as a whole. And he pleads for God to intervene in the present. That David is even addressing God in the midst of his agony demonstrates his faith in the fact that what he is experiencing matters to God.

And then, the psalm drastically shifts its tone in the last portion of verse 21. David's prayers have been answered. His cries have been heard. God did not hide Himself from David but came to his aid. In response, David praises God and calls the people to join in his celebration. David's suffering does not have the final word in this psalm; deliverance and celebration do. David invites us to remember that even in our trials, God hears our cries, and He will act.

> When going through a hard season, why do you think it is so important to reflect on the ways God has been faithful to us in the past?

Mark it Up: New Testament Passage

Having looked at Psalm 22, we turn now to consider Matthew 27:45–50, which records Jesus hanging on the cross and quoting the first verse of Psalm 22. Read this passage in Matthew multiple times and annotate, or mark up, the text as you read. For tips and examples on annotating, see pages 204–215.

> Highlight any words or phrases that point to Christ.

> Make note of any attributes of God seen in the text.

> Circle the words taken from Psalm 22.

> Underline any words that indicate the agony Jesus is feeling.

> What similarities do you see between David's experiences in Psalm 22 and what Jesus is experiencing here?

MATTHEW 27:45-50

⁴⁵ From noon until three in the afternoon, darkness came over the whole land.

⁴⁶ About three in the afternoon Jesus cried out with a loud voice,

"*Elí, Elí, lemá sabachtháni?*" that is, "My God,

my God, why have you abandoned me?"

⁴⁷ When some of those standing there heard this, they said,

"He's calling for Elijah." ⁴⁸ Immediately one of them ran and got a sponge,

filled it with sour wine, put it on a stick, and offered him a drink.

⁴⁹ But the rest said, "Let's see if Elijah comes to save him."

⁵⁰ But Jesus cried out again with a loud voice and gave up his spirit.

Make the Christ Connection

> Read Psalm 22:1–2 and Matthew 27:27–50.

In Jesus's day, crucifixion was a form of execution designed to be as humiliating and painful as possible. (It is where we get the term "excruciating" from.) Crosses were for the worst of criminals, which makes it all the more striking for Jesus, who was innocent—indeed, the only sinless person to ever live—to be found on one. In the midst of His agony, just before His death, Jesus takes up David's cry from Psalm 22: "My God, my God, why have you abandoned me?" (Psalm 22:1, Matthew 27:46).

> Why do you think Jesus quotes this psalm? What about it is appropriate to what He is experiencing?

_____

It is striking how many details from Psalm 22 are present in this passage of Matthew. Just as David had described his enemies dividing his garments and casting lots for them, so too does this happen for Jesus (Psalm 22:18, Matthew 27:35). Just as David's opponents mocked and shook their heads at him, Jesus is mocked as well (Psalm 22:7, Matthew 27:39). And like those who mocked David, Jesus's mockers assume that if God were so pleased with Him, Jesus wouldn't be suffering in the first place (Psalm 22:8, Matthew 27:43).

Jesus's suffering fully embodies Psalm 22—not just in these similar details but in its overall sense of agony. It is this agony that leads Him to cry out with the psalm's opening words. And yet Jesus's agony is far worse than what David experienced, for on the cross, Jesus is shouldering the full wrath of God against the sins of many. Jesus has experienced the love of His Father from "before the world's foundation" (John 17:24). But now—standing in as a substitute for sinners—He experiences something new: the judgment of His Father. This is a pain that transcends the already horrific physical pain of crucifixion.

> Though Psalm 22 expresses deep pain and sorrow, it is also a psalm that ends in victory, not despair. How might this add another level of significance to the fact that Jesus chooses to quote from this psalm?

David's suffering did not have the final word. Psalm 22 does not just describe pain but vindication. And in the same way, the gospels do not end with Jesus's death and burial but with His vindication. He is raised from the dead and has ascended to heaven to sit at God's right hand (Matthew 28:1–10, 16–20; Luke 24:50–53).

Before His arrest and crucifixion, Jesus had communicated to His disciples that He would be killed and then raised, but they struggled to accept it. Yet Jesus assured them that this must be His trajectory and that if they wanted to follow Him, they too must walk a similar path: suffering first, glory later (Matthew 16:21–27). As hard as it was to accept, the disciples—seeing their vindicated, risen Lord—were given boldness to accept the suffering of this life, knowing that glory awaits those who follow Jesus.

> How can remembering Jesus's trajectory—suffering now, glory later—encourage us in the trials of our lives?

Live it Out

> Read Psalm 22:1–2 and Matthew 27:45–50.

For many of us, if we are being honest, the language found in Psalm 22:1–2 is something that we may tend to believe good Christians just don't say. If someone in our church were to talk about how God is not answering their prayers, we might quickly shoot back with a verse about how God hears our prayers.

But the Bible does not just *allow* us to say things like this; it *encourages* it. Such laments are frequently found in Scripture, and they are an expression of faith, not a lack of it. The psalmists frequently take an honest inventory of life's pains on the one hand and remind themselves of what is true about God on the other. Laments live between those two realities and typically include "(1) an address to God, (2) a complaint, (3) a request, and (4) an expression of trust and/or praise" (Vroegop, 29).

Lament lives in the tension between what we know to be true of God and what we experience in this life. But it is important to recognize that God Himself has experienced this tension. Jesus—God in the flesh—experienced firsthand the agony of Psalm 22. Yet suffering was not the final word for Jesus. And because of this, it will not be the final word in our lives either.

Reflect on this week's verses as you answer the following questions.

> Are there times when you have minimized your pain when praying to God? How can the passages we have looked at this week encourage you to be more honest with Him?

Spend a few minutes reading through Hebrews 2:14–18. According to verse 18, what is Jesus able to do? What comfort can you take from this truth?

What truths about God can you remind yourself of when it feels like He is far or that He is not answering your prayers?

Psalms of Lament

Numerous psalms in the Bible are psalms of lament. These psalms express deep sorrow and honesty about life's struggles. But they also include reminders of God's character and His past actions, as well as pleas for Him to get involved in the author's current struggles. Notice the presence of these elements in Psalm 13.

PSALM 13

A Plea for Deliverance
For the choir director. A psalm of David.

How long, LORD? Will you forget me forever?

How long will you hide your face from me?

How long will I store up anxious concerns within me,

agony in my mind every day?

How long will my enemy dominate me?

David honestly voices his complaint to God, asking where He is.

Consider me and answer, LORD my God.

David asks God to get involved.

Restore brightness to my eyes;

otherwise, I will sleep in death.

My enemy will say, "I have triumphed over him,"

and my foes will rejoice because I am shaken.

But I have trusted in your faithful love;

my heart will rejoice in your deliverance.

I will sing to the LORD

David reminds himself of God's faithful love and expresses trust in Him.

because he has treated me generously.

More Examples of Psalms of Lament:
Psalms 5, 6, 10, 22, 44, 86, 88, 126, 142

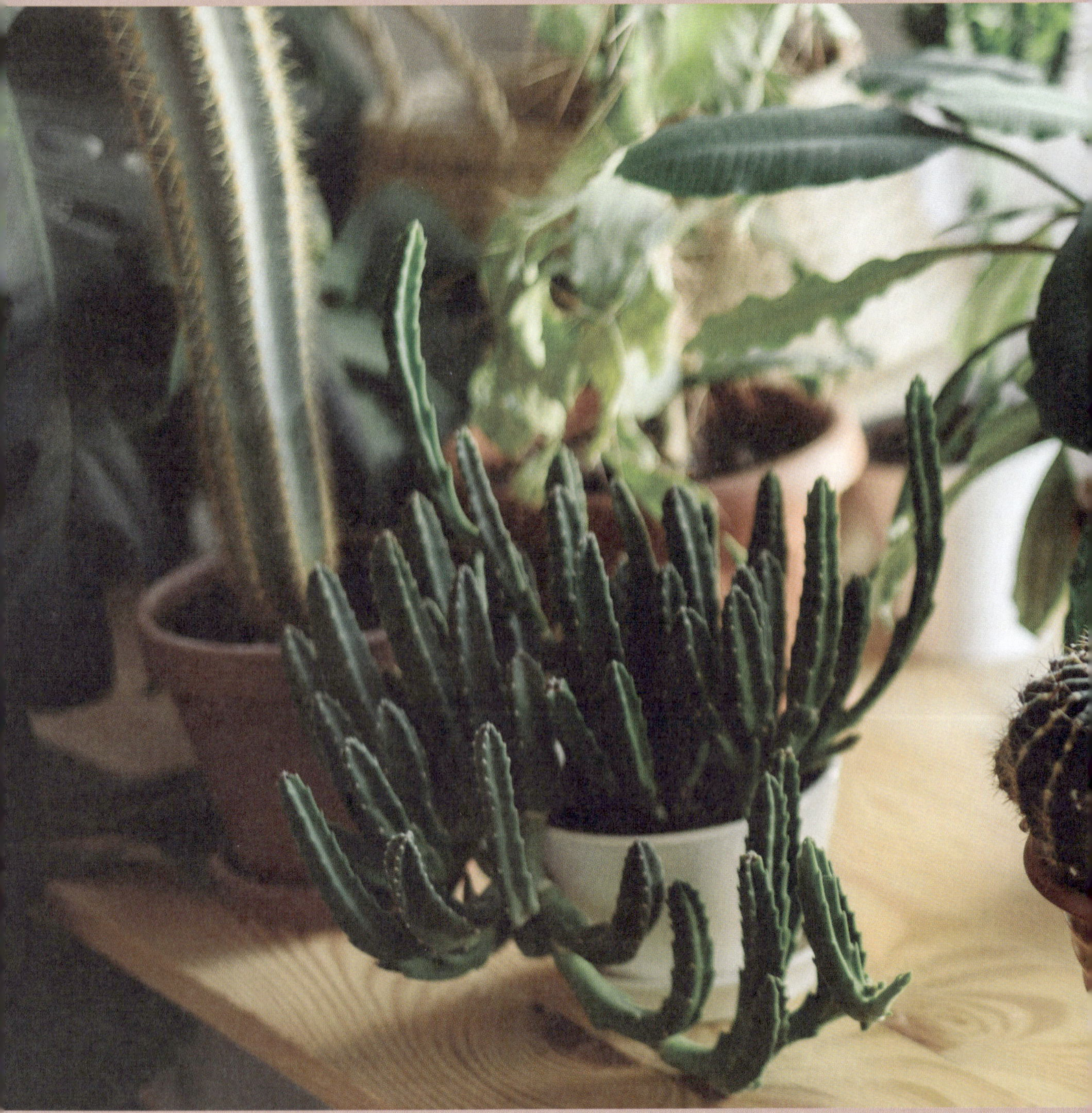

WEEK 31

Introduction

This week, you will read Psalm 110:1 and Matthew 22:41–46 and learn that Jesus reigns and rules at God's right hand. In response, you will be encouraged to worship Jesus and trust His reign as you wait for His kingdom to come in its fullness.

Mark it Up: Old Testament Passage

Today, we will begin studying Psalm 110:1, a verse that will help us learn how David prophesied about the coming Messiah. Read the passage two or three times and annotate, or mark up, the text as you read. For tips and examples on annotating, see pages 204–215.

Highlight any words or phrases that point to Christ.

Make note of any attributes of God seen in the text.

Circle the word "Lord" in the passage.

What is the one Lord proclaiming to the other?

Underline the word "enemies" in the verse.
Draw a line and write down who you think these enemies might be.

PSALM 110:1

[1] This is the declaration of the L ORD

to my Lord:

"Sit at my right hand

until I make your enemies your footstool."

Go Deeper

> Read Psalm 110:1.

David is known to be the greatest king in Israelite history. God chose David specifically to rule over Israel, and although David made mistakes, he was known to be a man after God's own heart (1 Samuel 13:14). He desired to listen to and obey the Lord, and He sought to lead Israel in their obedience to the Lord. But even though David was a great king, there was an even greater King who was coming after him. In Psalm 110, we hear about this great King from David's own lips.

> Now, read Psalm 110 in its entirety.

As we read Psalm 110, we see that this psalm describes a priestly King who has authority and victory. But it is not David who is being described. David speaks of two Lords in verse 1. The Hebrew word used for the first "Lord" is *Yahweh*, which is God's name, while the Hebrew word used for the second "Lord" is *adonai*, which can refer to either God or a human king. In Psalm 110, God is speaking to this other king, and because David refers to this other Lord as *his* Lord in verse 1, it is clear that David is not this king. Therefore, the priestly King whom God speaks to in this psalm is David's Lord. This means that this priestly King is greater than David.

> How do you see the King's greatness declared in this psalm?

_____
_____
_____
_____
_____

The words God speaks to this other "Lord" in Psalm 110:1 declare this Lord's greatness. God tells this person to sit at His right hand. To sit at the king's right hand would be the utmost honor and a sign of authority. Therefore, to sit at the right hand of the King of the universe would mean that this person, this priestly King, shares glory and authority with God Himself.

> Why do you think it is significant that this King shares glory and authority with God?

As we learned in Week 26, God formed a covenant with David, promising that from him would come a King who would rule on God's throne forever. This psalm speaks to this King, making Psalm 110 a Messianic Psalm, or a psalm that anticipates the Messiah to come.

So, while David would continue to be viewed as Israel's greatest king, he knew that there was someone to come who would surpass him in his greatness. Though David sat on an earthly throne, there was someone coming who would sit on a heavenly throne. Psalm 110:1 causes us to fix our eyes on this great King—the Messiah—who will reign in eternal glory.

> What do you think the Israelites' response would have been when they read this psalm? What truth do you think it holds for us today?

Mark it Up: New Testament Passage

Today, we will turn from Psalm 110:1 to study Matthew 22:41–46. As we do, we will learn how Jesus is the promised Messiah who is seated at the right hand of the Father. Read the passage two or three times and annotate, or mark up, the text as you read. For tips and examples on annotating, see pages 204–215.

Highlight any words or phrases that point to Christ.

Make note of any attributes of God seen in the text.

Who is Jesus talking to in this passage?

What is the answer to Jesus's first question in verse 42?

According to this passage, who is David calling "Lord"?

MATTHEW 22:41–46

⁴¹ While the Pharisees were together, Jesus questioned them, ⁴²

"What do you think about the Messiah? Whose son is he?"

They replied, "David's."

⁴³ He asked them, "How is it then that David,

inspired by the Spirit, calls him 'Lord':

⁴⁴ The Lord declared to my Lord,

'Sit at my right hand

until I put your enemies under your feet'?

⁴⁵ "If David calls him 'Lord,' how, then, can he be his son?" ⁴⁶ No one was able

to answer him at all, and from that day no one dared to question him anymore.

Make the Christ Connection

> Read Psalm 110:1 and Matthew 22:41–46.

The Jews waited years for God to fulfill His promise to bring the Messiah. They thought that this Messiah would come as a mighty victor who defeated the Israelites' enemies. But the Messiah who God sent was different. Yes, He was a great King. Yes, He would have victory. However, He would accomplish His victory through a humble death on the cross, revealing how God's kingdom is not about gaining power but giving it away. In Matthew 22:41–46, Jesus uses Psalm 110:1 to teach that the Messiah would be different from the people's expectations, pointing to Himself as this promised Messiah.

In Matthew 22, the Pharisees have been trying to test Jesus and discredit Him. But Jesus turns things around and questions the Pharisees themselves. Jesus questions the Pharisees by using Psalm 110:1, a psalm that the Pharisees know well because of its Messianic emphasis. Jesus challenges the Pharisees by asking them why David calls the Messiah "Lord" in this psalm.

The Pharisees, like many other Jews, believe that the Messiah will be someone exactly like David: a mighty warrior king. And because they know the Messiah will come from David's line, they believe that David will be greater than the Messiah, just as a father has more authority and significance than his son. But, as Jesus explains, since David calls the Messiah his "Lord," David demonstrates that he is, in fact, inferior to the Messiah. This truth silences the Pharisees, and they refuse to ask Jesus any more questions.

> Why do you think this truth silences the Pharisees? How is what Jesus is saying different from their expectations and beliefs about the Messiah?

While Jesus does not specifically speak of Himself in this passage, what Jesus reveals to the Pharisees is significant in light of who Jesus is and what He will do. Jesus is the promised Messiah, which means that Jesus is the One to whom God is speaking in Psalm 110. It was Jesus whom David prophesied about through the inspiration of the Spirit (Matthew 22:43). Therefore, Jesus is the fulfillment of the priestly King we read about in Psalm 110.

> Read Hebrews 10:11–13 and Romans 8:34. What do these verses say Jesus has done and is doing?

_____

_____

_____

_____

_____

_____

_____

_____

_____

_____

_____

_____

Many of the Jewish people rejected that Jesus was the promised Messiah. They refused to believe that Jesus was God's Son who had come to bring salvation. But even though the people did not believe, Jesus allowed Himself to be put to death on the cross. While such a death would seem like defeat, it was God's plan. Three days later, God raised Jesus from the grave, declaring Christ's victory over sin and death. Jesus then ascended to the Father, where He is now currently ruling and reigning at God's right hand. And one day, Jesus will return to bring God's kingdom in its fullness, and all of His people will worship Him with joy forever.

> Read Acts 5:30–31 and praise God for the truth that these verses proclaim.

Live it Out

> Read Psalm 110:1 and Matthew 22:41–46.

David's words from thousands of years ago ring true today, for Jesus sits on the throne at the right hand of the Father. Such a position boasts of Jesus's greatness and glory. And such truth reminds us that right here and now, Jesus sits on the throne. Jesus is ruling and reigning over all things, which is a great comfort to us as we live in this broken world. Though we may live under the earthly reign of human rulers, Jesus is still the ultimate King. Because Jesus is the ultimate King, we can trust Him and His control, knowing that He is greater than any worldly authority.

Jesus's lordship encourages us to marvel at His greatness and give Him the worship He deserves. His lordship also motivates us to look ahead to the day when He will return. Even though Jesus has ushered in God's kingdom, the kingdom has not yet come in its fullness. But when Jesus returns, He will establish His reign on earth, bringing God's kingdom in its fullness and removing all sin and evildoers from the world. While we wait for this day, we do so with hope and joy as we consider and worship our great King who rules on high.

Reflect on this week's verses as you answer the following questions.

> How does Jesus being at the right hand of God impact your everyday life?

In what ways does remembering Christ's rule and reign give you hope for the future?

How can you point others to Christ's greatness?

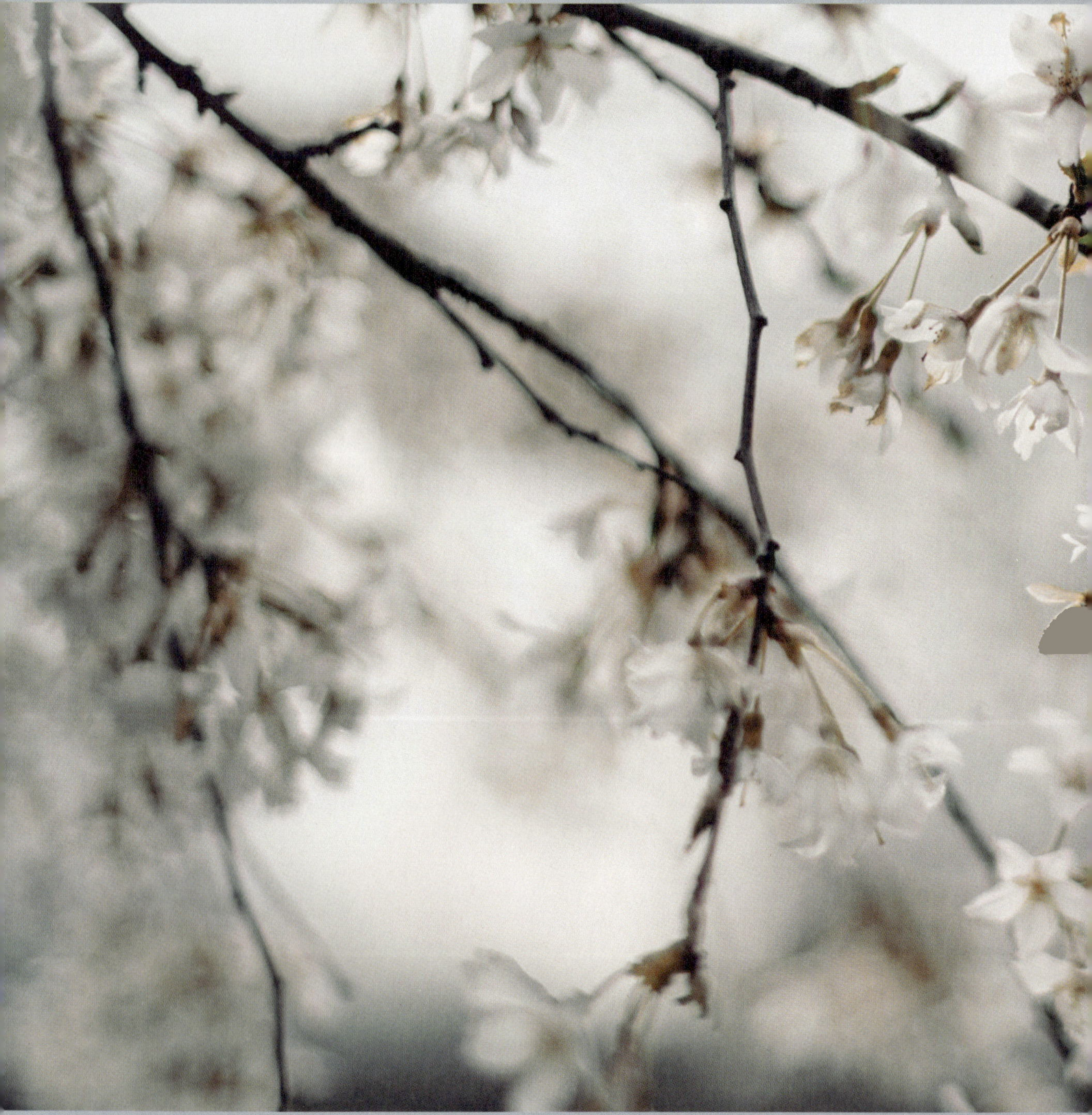

WEEK 32

Introduction

This week, we will trace the priesthood of Melchizedek through Psalm 110:4 and Hebrews 7:11–17. In response, we will be encouraged to place our faith in Jesus as our true and better High Priest. We will also be encouraged to rejoice in Christ's ability to be a High Priest forever, entering the Holy of Holies on our behalf, having made atonement for our sins once and for all.

> ATONEMENT:
> *The act of making amends for wrongdoing or sin.*

Mark it Up: Old Testament Passage

We begin this week with a study of Psalm 110:4, exploring Jesus's role as our Great High Priest. Read the passage two or three times and annotate, or mark up, the text as you read. For tips and examples on annotating, see pages 204–215.

Highlight any words or phrases that point to Christ.

Make note of any attributes of God seen in the text.

Underline the word "priest." What do you already know about the priesthood in ancient Israel?

Circle the word "forever." What do you think makes this word significant to the passage?

Make a note of any references to God's actions in the text.

PSALM 110:4

[4] The Lord has sworn an oath and will not take it back:

"You are a priest forever

according to the pattern of Melchizedek."

Go Deeper

> Read Psalm 110.

As we discussed last week, Psalm 110 is a Messianic Psalm, meaning that it points to the future coming Savior who is Jesus Christ.

> As you read Psalm 110, what Messianic themes do you see?

In this psalm, the author, King David, references an ancient figure named Melchizedek. We are first introduced to Melchizedek in Genesis 14 after Abraham defeats Chedorlaomer, a foreign king who has taken Abraham's nephew Lot captive (Genesis 14:1–16). Melchizedek gives Abraham a meal and gives glory to God for Abraham's victory. And in response, Abraham gives a tenth of all that he has to Melchizedek (Genesis 14:18–20).

> Read Genesis 14:18–20. What details about Melchizedek, if any, stand out to you?

Consisting of only three verses, Abraham's interaction with Melchizedek may seem short and insignificant, but it bears a great importance as we progress through the biblical narrative. We know that after God delivers the Israelites out of slavery in Egypt, He establishes a priesthood through the tribe of Levi that is required to enter the presence of God to make atonement for the people's sin (Exodus 29).

> What do you think King David meant when he used the phrase "the pattern of Melchizedek" in Psalm 110:4? How was Melchizedek's priesthood different from that of the Levitical priests?

Melchizedek served as a priest before the Levitical priesthood was established. Not only this, but Melchizedek was also a king who served before the formal kingship was established through the tribe of Judah. Just like his priesthood, Melchizedek's kingship is mysterious. Scripture does not say much about his role, but we know that Melchizedek was a king in Jerusalem. In this way, his kingship foreshadows the Davidic kingship that God would establish later in redemptive history.

David's mention of Melchizedek in Psalm 110 causes us to wonder about Melchizedek's significance in the biblical story. David speaks of a priest who remains forever. However, we know that all of the Levitical priests eventually died and were replaced by new priests. None of them lived forever. As we progress through our examination of Scripture this week, we will begin to have a clearer understanding of Melchizedek, the priest-king.

> Write a prayer of gratitude to God for giving us His Word. Ask Him to open your mind to understand what is being communicated through today's passage.

Mark it Up: New Testament Passage

Hebrews 7 reintroduces us to Melchizedek, whom we first read about in Psalm 110. In this passage, we will see how Melchizedek's priesthood points us to Jesus. Read Hebrews 7:11–17 two or three times and annotate, or mark up, the text as you read. For tips and examples on annotating, see pages 204–215.

Highlight any words or phrases that point to Christ.

Make note of any attributes of God seen in the text.

Circle the word "priesthood." Why would there be a need for another priest like Melchizidek?

What are some similarities between Melchizidek and Jesus?

HEBREWS 7:11–17

¹¹ Now if perfection came through the Levitical priesthood (for on the basis of it the people received the law), what further need was there for another priest to appear, said to be according to the order of Melchizedek and not according to the order of Aaron? ¹² For when there is a change of the priesthood, there must be a change of law as well. ¹³ For the one these things are spoken about belonged to a different tribe. No one from it has served at the altar. ¹⁴ Now it is evident that our Lord came from Judah, and Moses said nothing about that tribe concerning priests.

¹⁵ And this becomes clearer if another priest like Melchizedek appears,

¹⁶ who did not become a priest based on a legal regulation about physical descent but based on the power of an indestructible life. ¹⁷ For it has been testified:

You are a priest forever

according to the order of Melchizedek.

Make the Christ Connection

> Read Psalm 110 and Hebrews 7.

As we have learned, Psalm 110 is a Messianic Psalm that is meant to foreshadow the coming Messiah: Jesus Christ. When we studied Psalm 110:4 earlier in the week, we explored the priesthood of Melchizedek by examining Abraham's interaction with Melchizedek in Genesis 14. Now, as we turn to the New Testament, Hebrews 7 helps us continue to understand Melchizedek's unique role in the story of Scripture as this chapter sheds a dazzling light on his priesthood and what it symbolizes.

In Hebrews 7, we learn that Melchizedek's role as a priest and a king foreshadowed the superior priesthood and kingship of Jesus Christ. We see Melchizedek's legitimacy as a king-priest—as well as the superiority of his priestly order—through the fact that he received a tithe from Abraham, the patriarch and father of the Levitical line (Hebrews 7:4). It is worth noting, as we did on Day 2, that Melchizedek did not come from the Levitical line of priests as the tribe of Levi had not yet been established. However, the author of Hebrews teaches us that because Melchizedek's lack of having a Levitical genealogy did not prevent him from collecting Abraham's tithe, then neither can it prevent Jesus from serving as the perfect High Priest. Jesus is a High Priest in the order of Melchizedek, yet His priesthood is eternal (Hebrews 7:17). Unlike the Levitical priests who had to enter the temple over and over again to atone for sin and who eventually died, Jesus atoned for sin once for all time. Jesus lives forever in the presence of God as our eternal High Priest.

> Read Hebrews 7:23–24. How is Jesus able to remain a priest forever?

Jesus is the true and better Melchizedek. Jesus is not from the tribe of Levi, which God established to be the line of the priests, starting with Aaron. Instead, Jesus is from the tribe of Judah, which was established as the line of the kings in Genesis 49:10. In this way, Jesus is not only a priest but a king, just as Melchizedek was described as both "king of Salem" and "priest of God Most High" in Genesis 14:16. Yet Jesus is the true and better priest-king—the true and better Melchizedek.

> How is Jesus's priesthood better than that of the Levitical priests?

Hebrews 7 teaches us that, through Jesus, we have a better hope than what was given under the Law. While the Law and the Levitical priesthood could not save or perfect us, in Christ, we have a sure hope that our sins are atoned for forever (Hebrews 7:27). Not only is Christ a high priest now and forevermore, just as Melchizedek was installed as priest and king outside of the Levitical priesthood, so Christ has been installed as priest before time began. Through the oath that God made in Psalm 110, which spoke of an eternal high priest, we are given Jesus Christ as a permanent priest (Hebrews 7:22–24).

> Review Psalm 110:4. How does Jesus's priesthood follow "the pattern" of Melchizedek?

Live it Out

> Read Psalm 110:4 and Hebrews 7:11–17.

When we consider the implications of Christ's eternal priesthood for our own lives, we have much to be grateful for. Under the Law, the Levitical priests would have to enter the temple over and over again to atone for their own sin and the sins of the Israelites. Moreover, when each of these priests died, another priest would have to take his place. But because of Jesus, we no longer depend on sinful men to make atonement for us.

Because Jesus defeated death and is seated at the right hand of God (Hebrews 12:2), He remains a priest forever. Christ's sacrifice was enough to atone for our sin and the sin of the whole world. We can be encouraged to rejoice in Christ's ability to be a high priest forever, entering the Holy of Holies on our behalf to make atonement for our sins. We can praise God that we have a High Priest who will never die! Along with the Hebrew people to whom the book of Hebrews was written, we are inspired to place our faith in the true, better, and eternal High Priest and to remember Christ's superiority above all.

Reflect on this week's verses as you answer the following questions.

> In what ways is Jesus the true and better Melchizedek?

What are the benefits of having a priest who will not die?

Write out a brief prayer, praising God for His superiority above all other priests, prophets, and kings and reflecting on what this means for your life today.

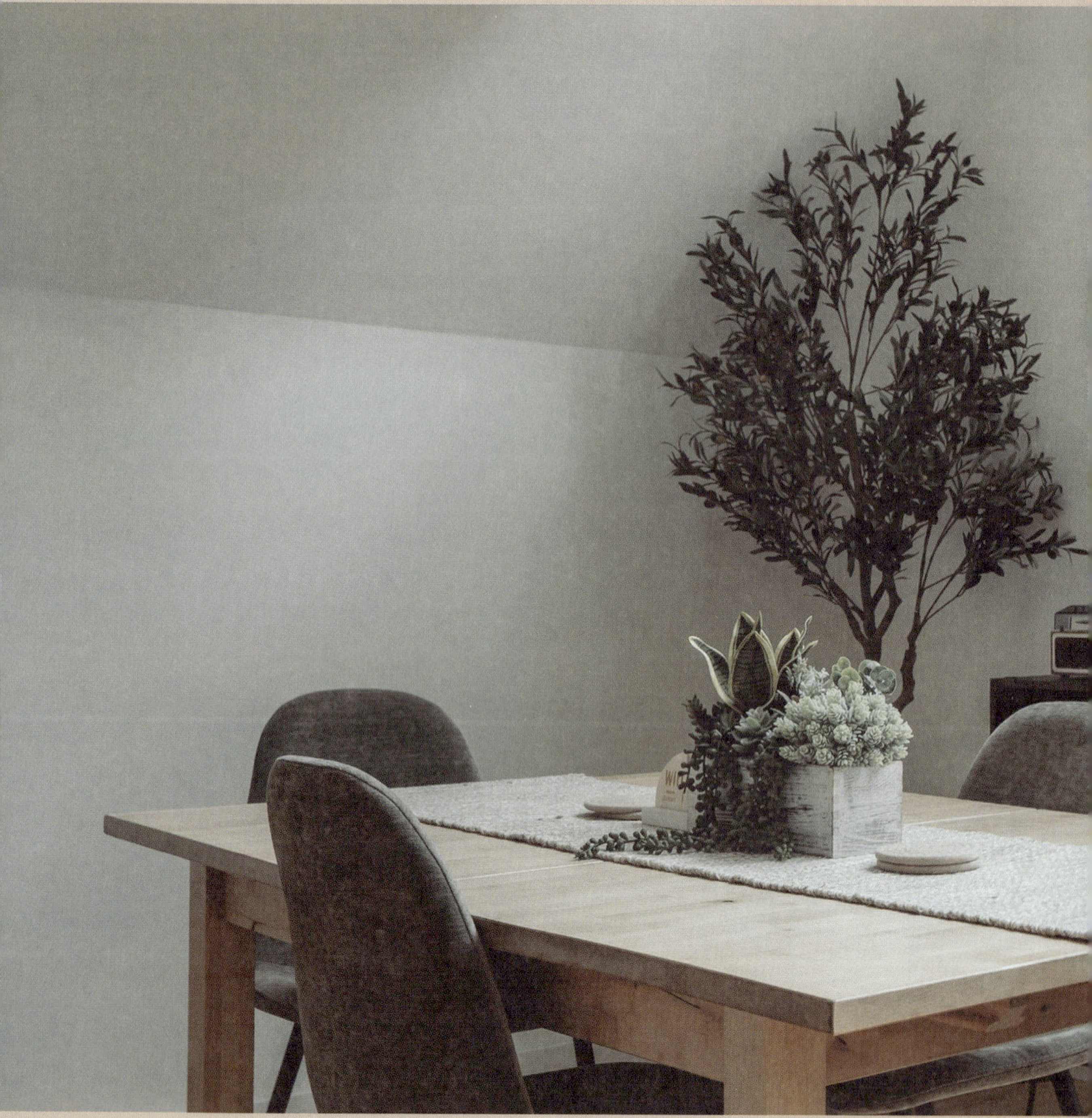

WEEK 33

Introduction

This week, we will study the theme of wisdom in Proverbs 1:7 and Colossians 2:2–3. We will learn about the human inclination to folly and see that true wisdom is found only in Jesus. In doing so, we will be encouraged to seek God's wisdom—rather than the wisdom of the world—by knowing and following Christ.

Mark it Up: Old Testament Passage

Today, we will begin our study of Proverbs 1:7 and see that true wisdom is found in Christ. Read the passage multiple times and annotate, or mark up, the text as you read. For tips and examples on annotating, see pages 204–215.

Highlight any words or phrases that point to Christ.

Make note of any attributes of God seen in the text.

Circle any occurrences of the word "wisdom" or related words.

Read Job 28:28, Psalm 111:10, Proverbs 9:10, and Proverbs 15:33. Returning to today's passage, underline the phrase you see repeated from these other passages.

Read Proverbs 1:1–7 in your Bible. Then, in the margin of this study, list any other words you see related to wisdom, knowledge, or instruction in these verses.

PROVERBS 1:7

⁷ The fear of the Lord

is the beginning of knowledge;

fools despise wisdom and discipline.

Go Deeper

Read Proverbs 1:1–7.

The book of Proverbs—as we learn in Proverbs 1:2—is written so that its readers can learn wisdom. Proverbs is one of the books of the Bible in the wisdom literature genre. The books in this genre (Job, Psalms, Proverbs, Ecclesiastes, and Song of Songs) are concerned with developing wisdom in God's people, and Proverbs perhaps most famously fulfills this purpose.

> **WISDOM:**
> *Biblically defined, wisdom is the ability to think and live in a godly and flourishing way. It begins with the fear of the Lord—acknowledging Him for who He is and submitting to His will.*

Read Proverbs 1:1–7 again slowly. How do you think the Bible defines wisdom?

_____

_____

_____

Notice the qualities listed in the passage: wisdom, discipline, and insight (1:2); prudence, righteousness, justice, and integrity (1:3); knowledge and discretion (1:4); listening, learning, and obtaining guidance (1:5). These are qualities we all likely admire, and all of them are captured by the term "wisdom." The book of Proverbs is written to aid God's people in this wisdom in themselves.

At the heart of this book is the statement in Proverbs 1:7 that wisdom (or knowledge) begins with the fear of the Lord. This truth is found all across the pages of Scripture (Job 28:28; Psalm 111:10; Proverbs 9:10, 15:33). What this means is that true wisdom can only be found through knowing God and acknowledging Him for who He is in all His glory, holiness, and authority.

Therefore, we should not think of Proverbs as a step-by-step guide to being wise or as a book of guarantees from God. Instead, we should read this book as an ideal description of the life of someone who fears the Lord. In other words, the instructions and rewards we find in the book should be understood as the way things ought to be—if the world had not been tainted by sin and brokenness. But the world is broken, humans do not fear the Lord, and wisdom has to contend with folly for the affection of our hearts.

Read Proverbs 1:7 again. Considering this verse and what you have learned about wisdom so far, how would you define folly?

FOLLY:
The quality of seeking one's own will and despising correction and instruction, especially from God.

We often consider folly—or foolishness—to be a lack of intelligence or stupidity, but Scripture does not describe it this way. Folly in Proverbs is the quality of those who are against God and His will—the ignorant and the mockers (Proverbs 1:22), those who despise wisdom and knowledge (Proverbs 1:7). Anyone who chooses their own will, their own knowledge, and their own desires over God's is considered a fool.

Are God's people more prone to wisdom or folly?

The Old Testament tells us the story of human rebellion against God. From Adam and Eve in the garden (Genesis 3) to the people of Israel at Mount Sinai (Exodus 32), humans choose to turn from God and disobey His commands time and time again. Since the Fall, the human heart has been prone to disobedience, rebellion, and selfishness—we are all prone to folly.

Thankfully, God is well aware of this propensity within the human heart, and He does not abandon His creatures to their folly. Although the story of the Bible is the story of human rebellion, it is also the story of God's faithfulness and His redemption of the human heart—redemption that ultimately comes through Jesus Christ.

Mark it Up: New Testament Passage

Today, we are studying Colossians 2:2–3. Through this passage, we will see how true biblical wisdom is found in Christ. Read Colossians 2:2–3 multiple times and annotate, or mark up, the text as you read. For tips and examples on annotating, see pages 204–215.

Highlight any words or phrases that point to Christ.

Make note of any attributes of God seen in the text.

Circle any words that are related to wisdom.

Underline any words or phrases that you have questions about.

Read the context that comes before these two verses (Colossians 1:1–2:1). Make note of the people to whom the different pronouns in the verse refer.

COLOSSIANS 2:2-3

² I want their hearts to be encouraged and joined together in love, so that they may have all the riches of complete understanding and have the knowledge of God's mystery—Christ. ³ In him are hidden all the treasures of wisdom and knowledge.

Make the Christ Connection

Read Proverbs 1:7 and Colossians 2:2–3.

Colossians is a letter written by the Apostle Paul to the church in Colossae — a church whose members he had likely not met in person. As both the persecution of Christians and the rise of false teachers threatened all churches across Asia Minor, Paul wrote to these Christians to remind them of the truths of Christ and encourage them to continue in their faith.

Read Colossians 1:9–10. What was Paul's prayer for this church?

At the beginning of his letter, Paul prays that the Colossian Christians might be filled with knowledge of God's will and with wisdom (Colossians 1:9) so that they may walk in a way that is pleasing to and worthy of God (Colossians 1:10). Paul's desire is that the members of this church would walk in the wisdom of God, obeying His will and living the way He intends them to.

But Paul is not telling them to find wisdom within themselves; he is quick to explain that God is the One who enables them to access this wisdom and all other forms of good because they have been rescued from darkness (Colossians 1:12–14). Then, in chapter 2, Paul says it explicitly: all the treasures of wisdom and knowledge are hidden in Christ (Colossians 2:3).

What does it mean that wisdom is "hidden" in Christ? Read Colossians 2:2–10.

Paul explains that there is a competing way of life that is contrary to God's wisdom—a philosophy (or a way of thinking and living) that is defined by meaninglessness and deception. Paul warns the church that they should avoid being taken captive by this way of life.

This worldly wisdom is representative of any ideology that informs thoughts or actions but is set against the wisdom of God, for all forms of worldly wisdom are based on human tradition and the elements of the world (Colossians 2:8).

This is why Paul says that true wisdom is hidden in Christ (Colossians 2:3). The wisdom of the world—in all its forms—is readily available to anyone who looks for it. It is embedded in our culture, our entertainment, and our sinful inclinations. But God's wisdom—true wisdom—can only be found in Christ.

> On Day 2 of this week, we learned that humans are prone to folly.
> How, then, can we be filled with God's wisdom that is hidden in Christ?

_____

_____

_____

_____

_____

_____

Proverbs 1:7 tells us that wisdom begins with the fear of the Lord and that fools despise instruction. We learned that this can be said of every human. We are sinful; we do not fear the Lord; we do not pursue wisdom; we are foolish; we despise instruction; we look to ourselves and to the world for guidance on how to think and live.

But Christ succeeded where we continuously fail. His life was defined by the fear of the Lord—by wisdom. While we seek our own will in even the most trivial instances, Christ submitted to the will of God in the most difficult instance by willingly going to the cross for the sins—the folly—of humanity (Luke 22:42).

Colossians 3:1–3 explains that those who trust in Christ are united to Him—for we have died with Him, have been raised with Him, and will be glorified with Him. Paul says that now, our lives are "hidden with Christ in God" (Colossians 3:3). We, too, are hidden with Christ. We are hidden with true wisdom. And with His power and His help, we too can fear the Lord and walk in wisdom.

Live it Out

Read Proverbs 1:7 and Colossians 2:3.

Wisdom is obtained through the fear of the Lord (Proverbs 1:7). But this week, we have learned that we are incapable of obtaining this wisdom in our own strength and are instead prone to folly—rebelling against God and seeking our own will. But Colossians 2:3 points us to Christ. True wisdom is found in Him, for He feared the Father and submitted to the Father's will.

Although this wisdom is hidden, Colossians 3:3 tells us that we who have placed our faith in Christ are also hidden with Him and, thus, have access to true wisdom. Now, then, we ought to resist folly and the wisdom of the world that is fighting for our affection and attention. Instead, we ought to seek to walk according to God's wisdom, which we have found in Christ.

Reflect on this week's verses as you answer the following questions.

What "worldly wisdom" have you encountered?

How does Jesus's life encourage and challenge you in your pursuit of wisdom?

Read Colossians 3:5–17 and make a list of the things of the world—i.e., the things of "your earthly nature" (verse 5)—and a list of the things of God. Make note of areas where you struggle. Pray and ask Christ to help conform you to the wisdom of God.

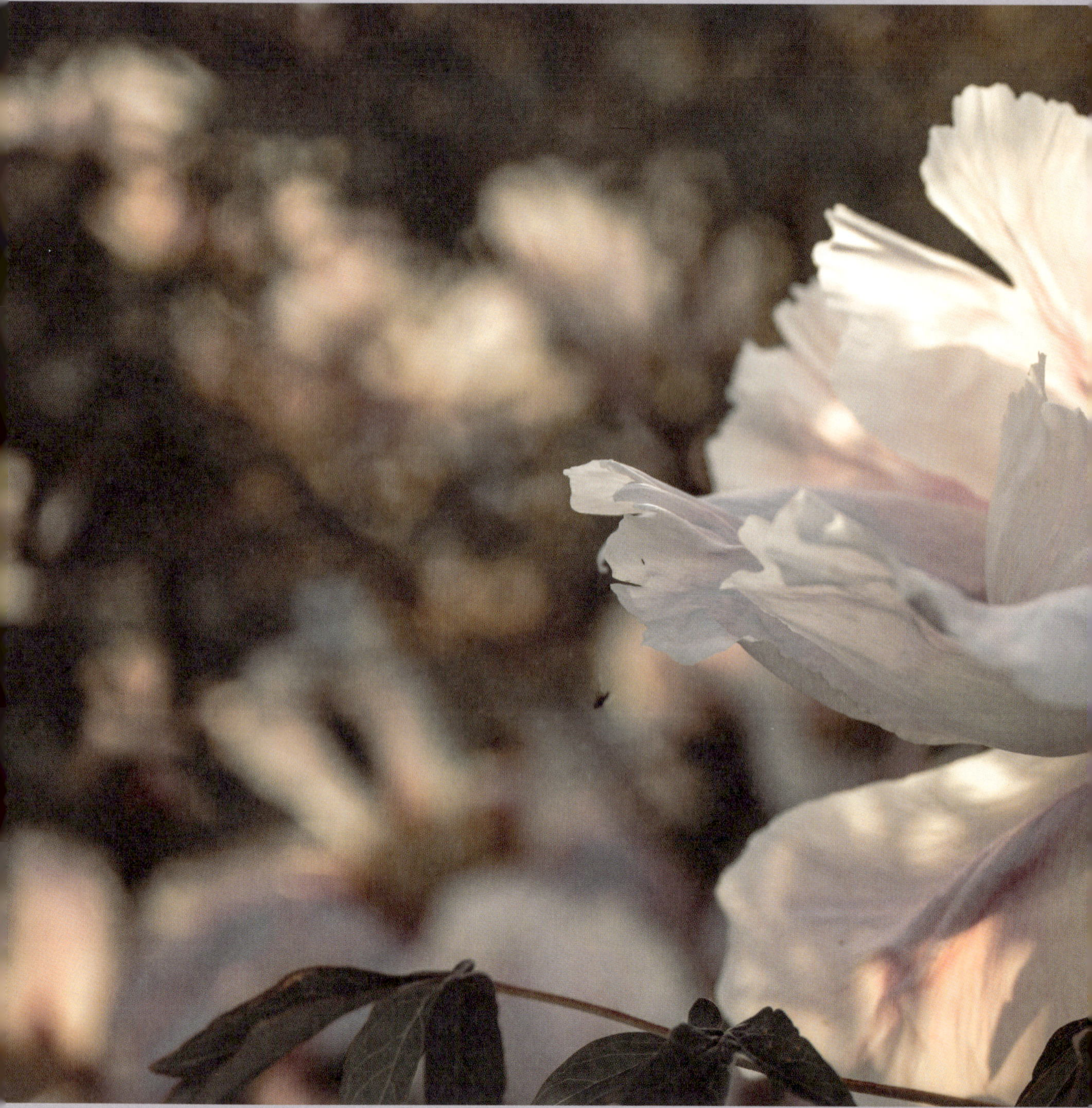

WEEK 34

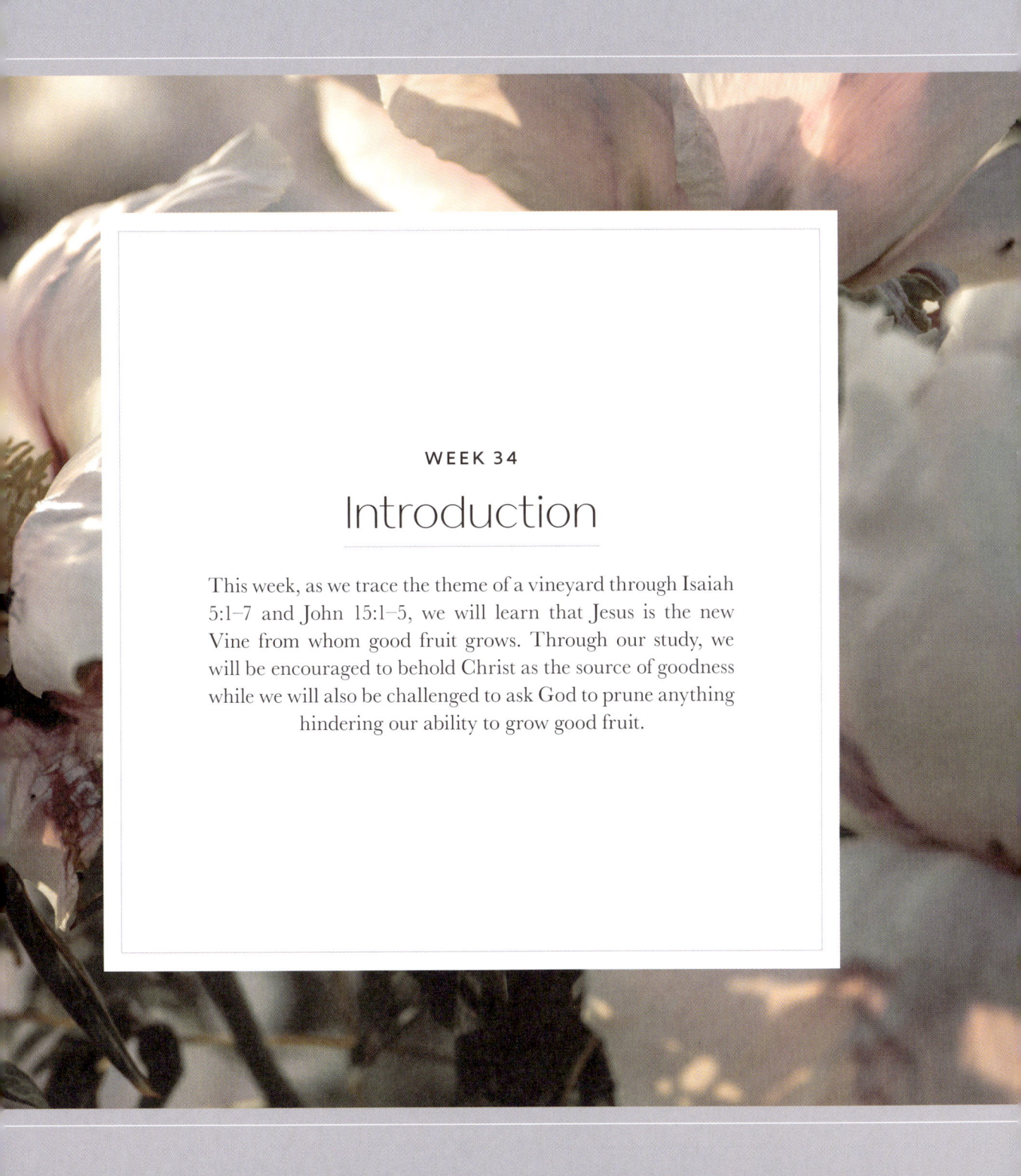

Introduction

This week, as we trace the theme of a vineyard through Isaiah 5:1–7 and John 15:1–5, we will learn that Jesus is the new Vine from whom good fruit grows. Through our study, we will be encouraged to behold Christ as the source of goodness while we will also be challenged to ask God to prune anything hindering our ability to grow good fruit.

Mark it Up: Old Testament Passage

Today, we will begin by studying Isaiah 5:1–7, which will prepare us to see how Jesus gives life to God's chosen vineyard and through Him alone, God's vineyard grows good fruit. Read the passage two or three times and annotate, or mark up, the text as you read. For tips and examples on annotating, see pages 204–215.

Highlight any words or phrases that point to Christ.

Make note of any attributes of God seen in the text.

Read verse 7. Now circle the words "the one I love" and "vineyard" in verse 1. Who does verse 7 reveal "the one I love" and the "vineyard" to be?

Highlight in a different color all the ways that God cared for His vineyard in verse 2. What does this reveal about God's character?

Read verse 7 again and underline the reason why God was disappointed in Israel and Judah.

Now look at verses 5–6 and circle God's response to His disappointment in His vineyard. Why does God respond this way?

Jesus is the new Vine from whom good fruit grows.

ISAIAH 5:1–7

¹ I will sing about the one I love,

a song about my loved one's vineyard:

The one I love had a vineyard

on a very fertile hill.

² He broke up the soil, cleared it of stones,

and planted it with the finest vines.

He built a tower in the middle of it

and even dug out a winepress there.

He expected it to yield good grapes,

but it yielded worthless grapes.

³ So now, residents of Jerusalem

and men of Judah,

please judge between me

and my vineyard.

⁴ What more could I have done for my vineyard

than I did?

Why, when I expected a yield of good grapes,

did it yield worthless grapes?

⁵ Now I will tell you

what I am about to do to my vineyard:

I will remove its hedge,

and it will be consumed;

I will tear down its wall,

and it will be trampled.

⁶ I will make it a wasteland.

It will not be pruned or weeded;

thorns and briers will grow up.

I will also give orders to the clouds

that rain should not fall on it.

⁷ For the vineyard of the LORD of Armies

is the house of Israel,

and the men of Judah,

the plant he delighted in.

He expected justice

but saw injustice;

he expected righteousness

but heard cries of despair.

Go Deeper

> Read Isaiah 5:1–7.

Isaiah's song describes a vineyard and its gardener but not just any vineyard and gardener. Isaiah's song is a parable in which God is the Gardener and His people (Israel and Judah) are His vineyard. God is the ultimate Caretaker, tending to His vineyard with love and a watchful eye from His watchtower. God expects good grapes to grow in His vineyard, and in anticipation of a good harvest, He has built a winepress to make the best wine. But even with the most tender of care, His vineyard produces sour grapes.

This vineyard parable reflects the nation of Israel's continued rebellion against God. Though God rescued them from slavery in Egypt, parted the Red Sea for their escape, and fed them in the wilderness—they continued to long for everything but God. Even so, God kept His promises and led them to the Promised Land.

In Deuteronomy 28, as they prepared to enter the Promised Land, Moses shared a list of blessings to be given if Israel would obey God and curses to be given if they failed to do so. Just as God expected His vineyard to yield good grapes, He desired to bless His people out of His covenant love.

> Read the blessings in Deuteronomy 28:1–14 and the curses in Deuteronomy 28:15–68. List out a few of these blessings and curses.

God promised to bless the people if they yielded good fruit—all the peoples on earth would know that Israel bears the Lord's name and would stand in awe of them. The nation's pursuits, their offspring, and their land would be blessed. As the Israelites prepared themselves to enter the Promised Land, God asked them to follow His commands. And God warned them of curses that would follow if they refused to obey.

Unfortunately, as Israel progressed in the Promised Land, when God looked for justice, He found injustice among His people. And when He sought righteousness, He heard cries of despair (Isaiah 5:7). His people sought satisfaction in other gods, in indulgence, and in earthly kings. Because of Israel's disobedience, God removed their hedge, tore down their walls, and eventually allowed them to be trampled by foreign nations and exiled from the Promised Land (Isaiah 5:5).

> Read Isaiah 5:8–16. What does God's judgment on His people teach us about His character?

The remainder of Isaiah 5 shows us the trampled vineyards—a place without God's blessing. The land no longer yields an abundant crop. Lovely houses now bear no inhabitants. Humanity is brought low. And worst of all, the people live their lives oblivious to the presence of God (Isaiah 5:12). By God's justice in the face of injustice, He is exalted. God demonstrates His holiness through His righteousness (Isaiah 5:16).

One day in the future, six to seven hundred years after Isaiah's words were penned, God's holiness would be embodied by a boy in a manger—a boy who would take upon Himself the curse of sin, a man who would gift His righteousness to the unrighteous, a man who would bring God's vineyard back to life, a vine that will always bear fruit and never be uprooted.

> Remember that, like the Israelites, we too are prone to take God's good gifts in vain. Ask Him to give you eyes to see His goodness today.

Mark it Up: New Testament Passage

Today, we will read John 15:1–5 and behold Jesus as the True Vine—the Redeemer of God's vineyard. Read the passage multiple times and annotate, or mark up, the text as you read. For tips and examples on annotating, see pages 204–215.

Highlight any words or phrases that point to Christ.

Make note of any attributes of God seen in the text.

Circle the three roles noted by Jesus in God's vineyard: the gardener, the vine, and the branches. Who do these represent?

Underline the repetition of the word "remain" in these verses. Why do you think Jesus emphasizes this word?

Highlight verse 5 in a different color. What is the promise of those who remain in Jesus, the True Vine?

JOHN 15:1-5

¹ I am the true vine, and my Father is the gardener. ² Every branch in me that does not produce fruit he removes, and he prunes every branch that produces fruit so that it will produce more fruit. ³ You are already clean because of the word I have spoken to you. ⁴ Remain in me, and I in you. Just as a branch is unable to produce fruit by itself unless it remains on the vine, neither can you unless you remain in me. ⁵ I am the vine; you are the branches. The one who remains in me and I in him produces much fruit, because you can do nothing without me.

Make the Christ Connection

> Read Isaiah 5:1–7 and John 15:1–5.

Imagine planting a garden, tilling the land, rejuvenating the soil, planting the finest seed, and watering the soil in perfectly proportioned amounts. You are doing everything you can for this garden. You water, and you watch. Yet weeks later, when buds should be blooming, only thorns grow. How would you feel?

God described His vineyard, the people of Israel, in this way. He protected them. He planted them in the Promised Land and nourished them with His presence. And still, His vineyard grew worthless grapes. God's people took His care in vain—squandering His good gifts and running after idols. And so, God removed His hedge of protection from them.

But He did not remove His promise.

> Read Isaiah 65:8–9. How did God plan to preserve His vineyard?

Because God's Word is truth, He cannot lie (Psalm 119:160). And because He cannot lie, He always keeps His promises. God promised Abraham that the world would be blessed through him (Genesis 12:3). He promised David that one day, a king from his lineage would reign forever (2 Samuel 7:13, 16). And in Isaiah 65:8–9, God promised to salvage grapes from His vineyard. He promised to save a remnant and settle them in His covenant love.

These good grapes would come from a good vine.

> Read John 15:1–17. How is God's vineyard able to be fruitful? What is different about this vineyard when compared to the first?

Jesus is the redemption of His Father's vineyard; He is the True Vine that cannot fail to bear fruit. As Jesus prepares His disciples for His coming death, resurrection, and ascension, He explains what it means to be a true disciple. To do so, He describes a vineyard scene in which He is the vine, His Father is the gardener, and His disciples are the branches. And to bear fruit, His disciples must be connected to Him, the True Vine.

Throughout these verses, Jesus repeats the words "remain" or "remains" eleven times. These words describe a fruit-bearing union that exists between Jesus and His followers—Jesus's life brings life to those who follow Him. His righteousness is extended to them by grace through faith. As Jesus was sinless, so too His disciples are counted sinless in His name. As Jesus is the Son of God, so too His disciples are adopted into God's covenant family.

Fruitfulness of the branches is entirely dependent upon their connection to the vine. Apart from Christ, Christ's followers can do nothing (John 15:5); we are withered branches, lifeless sticks. But in Christ, we are chosen and loved. In Christ, we can have joy and life everlasting.

Jesus is the life of God's vineyard. At the end of the age, when the harvest has come, God will collect new grapes grown from the True Vine and be delighted. Though His people once squandered His blessing, God did not build His winepress in vain (Isaiah 5:2). New wine flows forth in Jesus.

> Read John 10:10. Ask God to help you heed Jesus's advice and remain connected to Him, no matter the season or storm.

Live it Out

> Read Isaiah 5:1–7 and John 15:1–5.

This week, we have studied Israel's failure as God's chosen vineyard. God did all that He could for the vineyard; He planted the vines on a fertile hill, broke up the soil, and protected it. But still, the vineyard grew worthless fruit (Isaiah 5:2–4). Despite God's care for the nation, they chose to worship other gods and store their treasures on earth. And so God removed His hedge of protection and allowed them to be trampled by enemies.

But instead of giving up on His people, God planted a new vine, a vine that would never fail. Jesus is that True Vine. Branches depend upon a vine for sustenance, support, and fruitfulness. In the same way, followers of Christ depend upon Him.

If you are a follower of Christ, you depend upon Him for life. His Word nourishes your soul. His presence supports you through any season and storm. Just as a branch rests in the vine, you rest in Christ. As the vine provides the necessary nutrients to sustain growth, the Holy Spirit indwells you and gives you Christ's power to live in obedience and worship. If you are connected to the Vine, your life will bear fruit that glorifies the Gardener, your Father in heaven.

As you reflect upon Christ as the True Vine, remember that it is only through Him that you have life. The fullness of joy—of satisfaction, peace, and hope—can only be found by abiding in Christ. Remain in Him—go to Him for strength, guidance, mercy, and instruction. Remember that apart from Him, you can do nothing.

Reflect on this week's verses as you answer the following questions.

> What does God's redemption of His vineyard teach you about His character?

Would you say that you depend upon Christ? If so, for what? If not, what else do you depend upon in Christ's place?

What does it mean to remain in Christ? How might you better remain in Him in your current season?

Israel as a Fruitless Vine

In the Old Testament, the nation of Israel is sometimes compared to a vine. And often, it is a worthless vine they are being compared to—one that should have borne good fruit but did not. Jesus, on the other hand, is the True Vine (John 15:1) who produces good fruit.

Here is a sampling of verses from the Old Testament that carry the metaphor of Israel as a vine and ultimately point us toward our True Vine, Jesus Christ:

> You dug up a vine from Egypt;
> you drove out the nations and planted it.
> You cleared a place for it;
> it took root and filled the land.
> The mountains were covered by its shade,
> and the mighty cedars with its branches.
> It sent out sprouts toward the Sea
> and shoots toward the River.
>
> **PSALM 80:8–11**

> For the vineyard of the Lord of Armies
> is the house of Israel,
> and the men of Judah,
> the plant he delighted in.
> He expected justice
> but saw injustice;
> he expected righteousness
> but heard cries of despair.
>
> **ISAIAH 5:7**

> I planted you, a choice vine
> from the very best seed.
> How then could you turn into
> a degenerate, foreign vine?
>
> **JEREMIAH 2:21**

> Therefore, this is what the Lord God says, "Like the wood of the vine among the trees of the forest, which I have given to the fire as fuel, so I will give up the residents of Jerusalem. I will turn against them. They may have escaped from the fire, but it will still consume them. And you will know that I am the Lord when I turn against them. I will make the land desolate because they have acted unfaithfully." This is the declaration of the Lord God.
>
> **EZEKIEL 15:6–8**

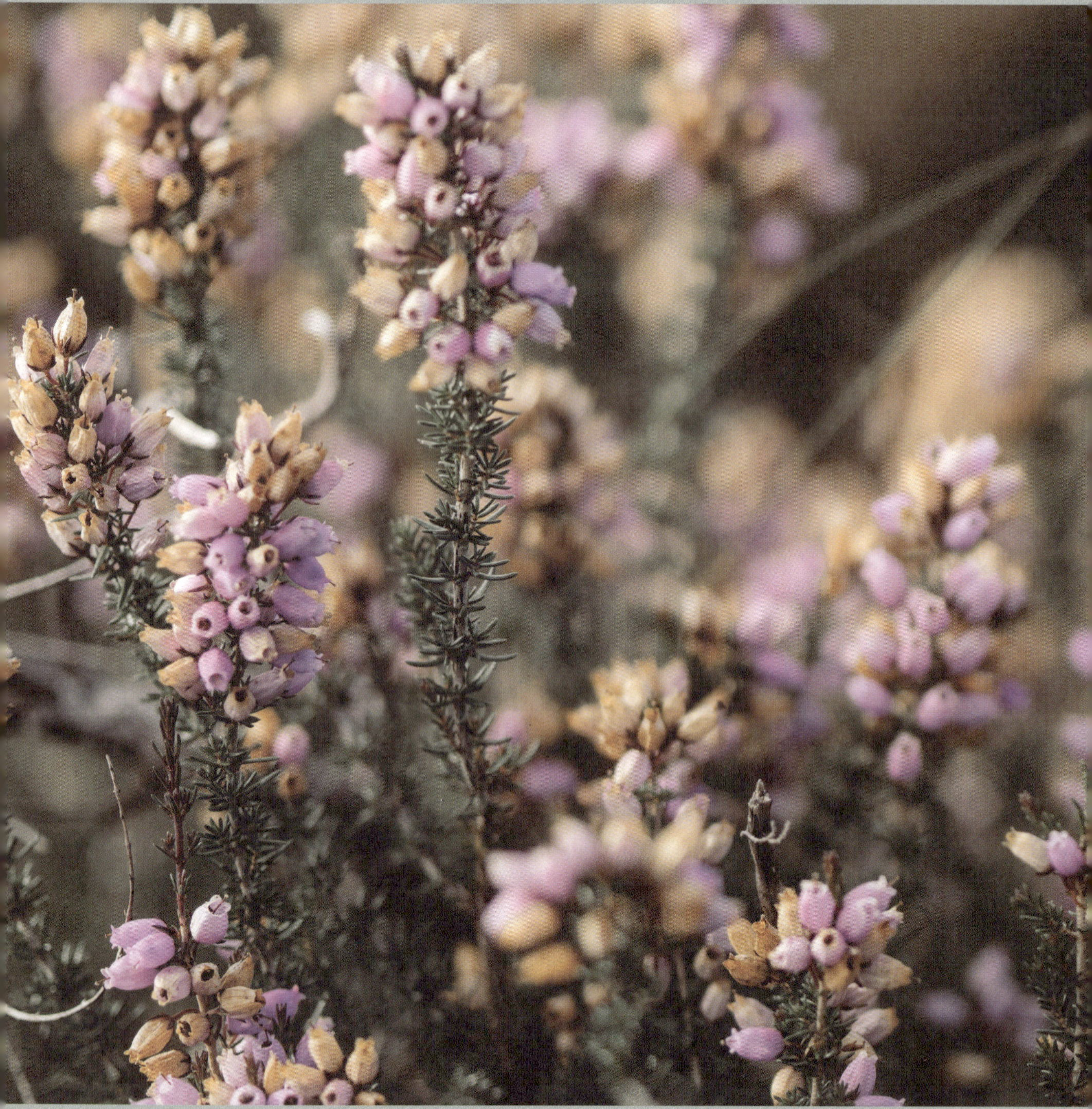

WEEK 35

Introduction

This week, we will consider Isaiah's prophecy of a child to come (Isaiah 7:10–14) and the ultimate fulfillment of that promise in the birth of Jesus (Matthew 1:21–23). In comparing these passages, we will see that Jesus is the long-awaited King who is faithful to God, and we will be encouraged to reflect on the fact that God has come near to us through Jesus and desires to have a relationship with us.

Mark it Up: Old Testament Passage

Today, we will begin our study of Isaiah 7:10–14, a prophecy spoken around six to seven hundred years before Jesus's birth. Read the passage multiple times and annotate, or mark up, the text as you read. For tips and examples on annotating, see pages 204–215.

Highlight any words or phrases that point to Christ.

Make note of any attributes of God seen in the text.

Underline God's words (spoken through the prophet Isaiah) to King Ahaz of Judah in verses 13–14.

Circle Ahaz's reply to God's message.

Read Isaiah 7:1–9. What has been happening up to this point in Isaiah 7? What is Ahaz afraid of?

Now, read Isaiah 7:15–17 and make a note of what you read in those verses regarding Isaiah's prophecy.

ISAIAH 7:10-14

[10] Then the L ORD spoke again to Ahaz: [11] "Ask for a sign from the L ORD your God—it can be as deep as Sheol or as high as heaven."

[12] But Ahaz replied, "I will not ask. I will not test the L ORD."

[13] Isaiah said, "Listen, house of David! Is it not enough for you to try the patience of men? Will you also try the patience of my God? [14] Therefore, the Lord himself will give you a sign: See, the virgin will conceive, have a son, and name him Immanuel."

Go Deeper

> Read Isaiah 7:1–17.

Editor's note: By this point in redemptive history, God's chosen nation has split into two separate kingdoms, with the larger kingdom of Israel to the north and the smaller kingdom of Judah to the south. Because Isaiah 7 contains a prophecy that Isaiah delivered to the southern kingdom's King Ahaz, in this entry, we will focus on the kingdom of Judah specifically.

The theme of trust runs throughout Isaiah 7–39. Specifically, in the face of military threats, will Judah's king trust in God to protect the nation as He promised? Or will the king depend on political alliances with other nations?

That is the issue with which the prophet Isaiah confronts Ahaz, king of Judah, in Isaiah 7:1–9. At this time, the threat of the Assyrian Empire is looming large. But the more immediate threat Ahaz faces comes from his closest neighbors to the north, Israel and Aram, which some Bible translations reference as Syria (Isaiah 7:1). These two nations have joined forces and are planning on invading Judah to install a king to join with them in an attempt to repel the Assyrians. So, option one is to endure a brutal invasion by Israel and Aram. Option two is to partner with them to take on the mighty Assyrian Empire.

Isaiah, however, presents Ahaz with option three: trust in God, not other nations, for protection. Ahaz is, after all, sitting on David's throne, a throne that God promised will endure forever (2 Samuel 7:16). Through Isaiah, God tells Ahaz that Israel and Aram's plan to invade will come to nothing, and He offers to give Ahaz a sign proving His presence with him.

> Can you sympathize with Ahaz's difficult position? How does he respond to God's offer of a sign?

Ahaz refuses to ask for a sign, for he has already made up his mind about what he will do. According to 2 Kings 16:7–9, Ahaz sends money to Assyria's king and begs for his help against Israel and Aram, effectively pledging himself and his kingdom to Assyria and not to God.

So, God decides to give Ahaz a sign anyway: a young woman will conceive and give birth to a child named "Immanuel." Before this child reaches a certain age, the lands of Israel and Aram, which Ahaz has so feared, will have been decimated by the Assyrians. But, because of Ahaz's foolish decision, the Assyrian threat will spill over into Judah as well, leaving very little food for its people and for the child (Isaiah 7:15, 18–25).

> What is ironic about Ahaz appealing to Assyria for help? In what ways is this decision counterproductive?

Tragically, the Assyrians—the very people Ahaz decided to turn to for help—end up devastating his kingdom, nearly destroying it completely. As such, Ahaz's faithlessness puts God's people at risk. The sign of Immanuel—meaning "God with us"—is thus a sign of judgment against Ahaz. But for others, it is a sign of hope. Though the land of Judah will be devastated, God will preserve a faithful remnant and be with them (Isaiah 6:13, 8:9–10, 10:20–22).

Immanuel, therefore, speaks to the failure of Judah's king but also to God's commitment to His people. And because of this commitment, God will one day send a faithful King to rule over His people, a King called "Wonderful Counselor, Mighty God, Everlasting Father, Prince of Peace" (Isaiah 9:6).

> Spend time thanking God for His promise to send a faithful King to rule over His people.

Mark it Up: New Testament Passage

Centuries after the events recorded in Isaiah 7, Matthew wrote his Gospel and showed how Isaiah 7:14 was ultimately fulfilled in the birth of Jesus. Read Matthew 1:21–23 multiple times and annotate, or mark up, the text as you read. For tips and examples on annotating, see pages 204–215.

> Highlight any words or phrases that point to Christ.

> Make note of any attributes of God seen in the text.

> Circle the meaning of Jesus's name.

> Underline any references you see to Isaiah 7.

> Read verses 20–21. Who is speaking, and who is being spoken to?

MATTHEW 1:21–23

[21] "She will give birth to a son, and you are to name him Jesus,

because he will save his people from their sins."

[22] Now all this took place to fulfill what was spoken

by the Lord through the prophet:

[23] See, the virgin will become pregnant

and give birth to a son,

and they will name him Immanuel,

which is translated "God is with us."

Make the Christ Connection

> Read Isaiah 7:10–14 and Matthew 1:1–25.

When King Ahaz entrusted his kingdom's security to Assyria instead of God, he ended up jeopardizing their security instead. He was a model of failed leadership. But so, too, were Judah's good kings. For example, Ahaz's son, Hezekiah, showed tremendous faith in God in the face of the Assyrian threat, and God miraculously delivered Jerusalem, Judah's capital city (Isaiah 36–37). Yet Hezekiah—in his pride—revealed the wealth and military capabilities of Judah to Babylon, the future enemies of the nation (Isaiah 39). Both the bad and even the good kings testified to the need for a king like the one described in Isaiah 9:6–7 and 11:1–2, a righteous king who would rule over God's people with wisdom and justice.

And it is such a King that we are introduced to in Matthew 1, which begins with reference to "Jesus Christ, the Son of David, the Son of Abraham" (Matthew 1:1).

> Why do you think Matthew includes a genealogy at the beginning of his Gospel? What purpose might it serve?

_____
_____
_____
_____

While it might not strike us as engaging, Matthew's genealogy is important. First, by tracing Jesus's descent from Abraham, Matthew links Jesus to God's promise to bless all nations through Abraham. And by tracing Jesus's descent from David, Matthew links Jesus with God's promise to sit one of David's descendants on his throne forever. Jesus is that descendant who would succeed where so many other kings had fallen short.

However, Jesus's birth is quite unusual. Before Mary and Joseph are officially wed, Mary is found to be pregnant. Joseph assumes the obvious and prepares to "divorce her secretly," but an angel comes to him and informs him that "what has been conceived in her is from the Holy Spirit" (Matthew 1:19–20). Despite being a virgin, she will give birth to a boy, and they are to name Him Jesus (Matthew 1:21).

> Many Jews at this time were looking for salvation—for someone to save them—from the Romans, who had occupied their land. What kind of salvation does Jesus offer? How does this salvation give us freedom?

Matthew sees in these events a deep connection with the Immanuel sign given to King Ahaz. Just as the child born in Isaiah's day communicated God's presence with His people, so too does Jesus—but in a far greater sense. Jesus, as the eternal Son of God who took on flesh, is quite literally God with us (Matthew 1:23). In his Gospel, John refers to Jesus as "the Word," writing that "in the beginning was the Word, and the Word was with God, and the Word was God" (John 1:1). A few verses later, he adds: "The Word became flesh and made his dwelling among us" (John 1:14).

Jesus is God with us. God has come near through Him. And this truth was not dampened when Jesus ascended into heaven, for after He ascended, He sent the Holy Spirit to indwell every Christian. Jesus the King has received all authority, and through the Spirit, He is with us "to the end of the age" (Matthew 28:18–20).

> How can the truth that "God is with us" (Matthew 1:23) encourage you this week?

Live it Out

> Read Isaiah 7:10–14 and Matthew 1:21–23.

Take a few minutes to read and reflect on the following passages:

> *I will take you as my people, and I will be your God.*
> **EXODUS 6:7A**

> *I will place my residence among you, and I will not reject you. I will walk among you and be your God, and you will be my people.*
> **LEVITICUS 26:11–12**

> *For we are the temple of the living God, as God said: I will dwell and walk among them, and I will be their God, and they will be my people.*
> **2 CORINTHIANS 6:16B**

> *Then I heard a loud voice from the throne: Look, God's dwelling is with humanity, and he will live with them. They will be his peoples, and God himself will be with them and will be their God. He will wipe away every tear from their eyes. Death will be no more; grief, crying, and pain will be no more, because the previous things have passed away.*
> **REVELATION 21:3–4**

Throughout Scripture, God's consistent heartbeat is to dwell with His people. And with the arrival of Jesus, "God with us," that is now a present reality for us. We have constant access to God's presence through prayer and the hope of dwelling with Jesus face-to-face forever on a new earth.

Reflect on this week's verses as you answer the following questions.

> When does God feel far from you? In these moments, what truths from this week can you remind yourself of?

Unlike King Ahaz and rulers all over the world today, Jesus is a perfect King who rules justly and who will hold all other rulers accountable. How can this comfort you in times of trial?

Write out a prayer, thanking God for not staying far off but coming near to us.

Messianic Prophecies in Isaiah

Born of a virgin
ISAIAH 7:14 — MATTHEW 1:21-23

Heir to David's throne
ISAIAH 9:6-7, 11:1, 10 — LUKE 1:32-33

Abused
ISAIAH 50:6 — MATTHEW 26:67

Exalted
ISAIAH 52:13 — JOHN 12:32

Suffering
ISAIAH 53:2-5 — MARK 15:15-19

Pierced for our sins
ISAIAH 53:5 — JOHN 19:34

Buried in a rich man's tomb
ISAIAH 53:9 — MATTHEW 27:57-60

> Therefore, the Lord himself
> will give you a sign:
> See, the virgin will conceive,
> have a son,
> and name him Immanuel.

ISAIAH 7:14

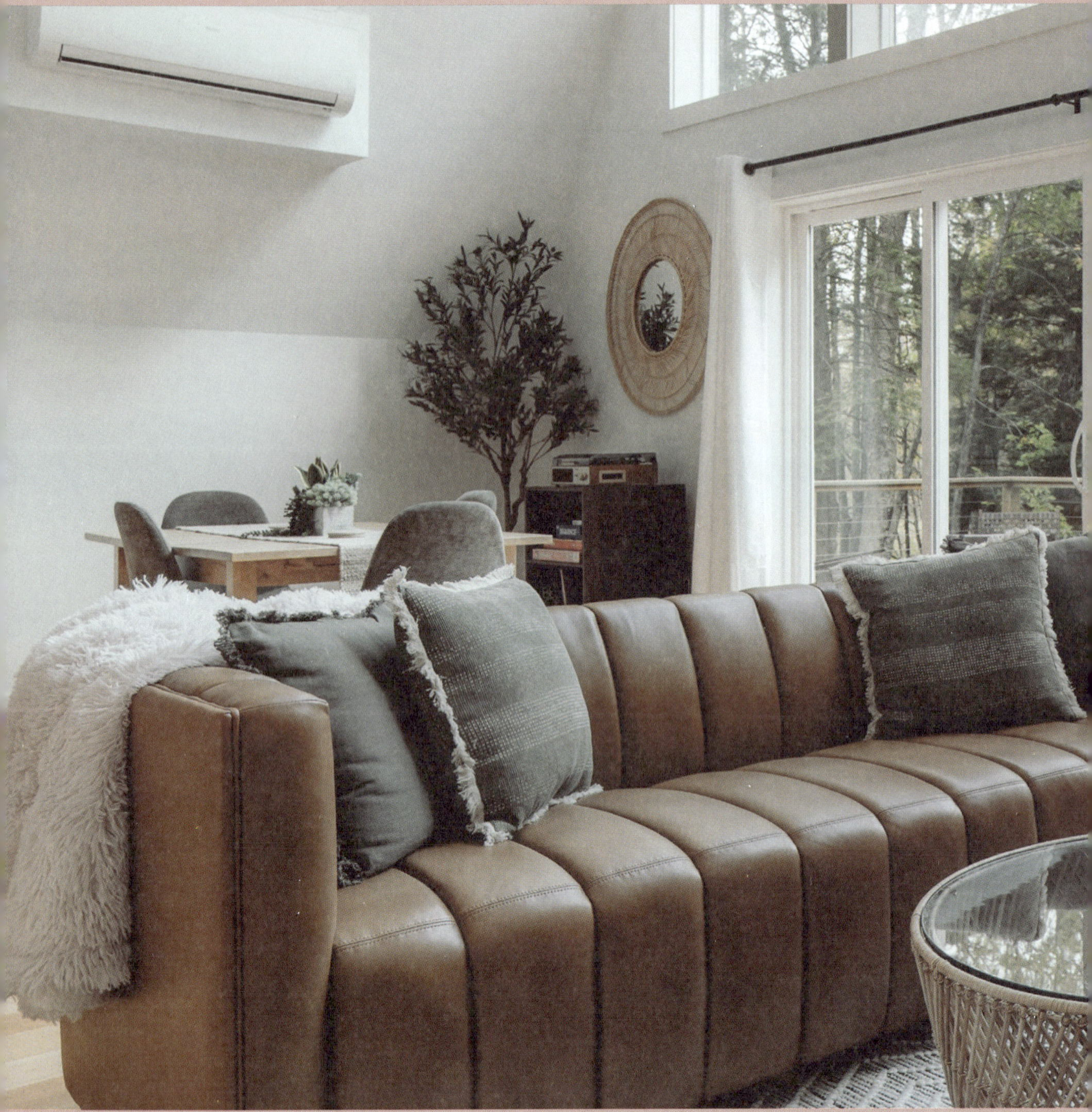

WEEK 36

Introduction

This week, by studying Isaiah 40:1–5, we will see Isaiah's prophecy of a messenger who would prepare the way for the Messiah. Then, as we turn to the New Testament, we will see how this prophecy was fulfilled in John the Baptist by studying Luke 3:1–6, 21–22. This will lead us to praise God for His faithfulness to His plan of redemption that ultimately culminates in Jesus Christ.

Every valley will be lifted up,
and every mountain and
hill will be leveled;
the uneven ground will
become smooth
and the rough places, a plain.

ISAIAH 40:4

Mark it Up: Old Testament Passage

Today, we will begin our study in Isaiah 40:1–5 and discover what the prophet has to say about the messenger who will prepare the way for the Messiah. Read the passage two or three times and annotate, or mark up, the text as you read. For tips and examples on annotating, see pages 204–215.

Highlight any words or phrases that point to Christ.

Make note of any attributes of God seen in the text.

Who is speaking in this passage? Who are they speaking to?

Underline the word "comfort." God tells Isaiah to announce a message of comfort to God's people. Why might Isaiah's announcement be comforting?

Circle the word "prepare." Who or what is Isaiah preparing the people for in verses 3–5?

Make a note of any references to God's actions in the text.

ISAIAH 40:1–5

¹ "Comfort, comfort my people,"

says your God.

² "Speak tenderly to Jerusalem,

and announce to her

that her time of hard service is over,

her iniquity has been pardoned,

and she has received from the Lord's hand

double for all her sins."

³ A voice of one crying out:

Prepare the way of the Lord in the wilderness;

make a straight highway for our God in the desert.

⁴ Every valley will be lifted up,

and every mountain and hill will be leveled;

the uneven ground will become smooth

and the rough places, a plain.

⁵ And the glory of the Lord will appear,

and all humanity together will see it,

for the mouth of the Lord has spoken.

Go Deeper

> Read Isaiah 40:1–5.

Have you ever had to relay difficult news to someone? The prophet Isaiah can relate. He is charged with delivering a heavy message to the people of Judah who are in danger of being exiled to Babylon as a result of their rebellion and disobedience to God. Isaiah does not shy away from pronouncing the sin of Judah. He reminds them of the covenant that God made with them and their obligation to obey Him—the obligation that they failed to keep.

Both the people of Judah and their leaders have acted in corruption. They have acted unjustly and sinned against God. They have heaped judgment upon themselves because of their disregard for the Lord's commands. Yet, in the midst of the troubling truths that the people receive from Isaiah, they also receive glimpses of the redemption that is to come. Though Isaiah must deliver bad news, he is also a carrier of hope.

> Why might the people of Judah be in need of a message of hope?

_____
_____
_____
_____
_____

During Isaiah's time, messengers, or heralds, were often sent out to pronounce significant news and information. In the same way, God uses Isaiah as this type of messenger. The message God speaks through Isaiah is weighty and worthy of this type of heralding. God sends Isaiah to announce the Lord's intent to draw near to His people again, despite their sin and rebellion. Though he speaks of Judah's coming destruction, Isaiah also speaks of Judah's future redemption. Isaiah's message will prepare the hearts of God's people to hear the Lord's voice and see God clearly, thus making the pathway for the Lord's coming smooth and level. Isaiah's prophecy is framed as a message of comfort and mercy for God's people. His words assure them that, after their exile, their sin will be pardoned (Isaiah 40:2).

What does verse 4 say will happen before the glory of the Lord appears?

As the people of Judah receive the message of future destruction, they are not left to believe that God will completely abandon them. In His kindness, God speaks through the prophet Isaiah a promise of His presence with them. Though Judah will eventually succumb to exile in Babylon, they can be comforted that God will not abandon them there. Not only is Judah given the promise that they will see the glory of God appear, but all humanity receives the hope of seeing God's glory (Isaiah 40:5).

How does Isaiah's message of hope affect us now? Reflect on God's promise of redemption and write a brief prayer, thanking God for His mercy.

Through Jesus,
we have the promise
of eternal life when we
place our faith in Him.

Mark it Up: New Testament Passage

In today's New Testament passages, we will learn about John the Baptist—the messenger about whom Isaiah prophesied—and how his ministry prepared the way for Jesus, the Messiah. Read Luke 3:1–6, 21–22 two or three times and annotate, or mark up, the text as you read. For tips and examples on annotating, see pages 204–215.

Highlight any words or phrases that point to Christ.

Make note of any attributes of God seen in the text.

Who is John the Baptist's father (Luke 3:2)?

Where was John the Baptist when the word of the Lord came to him (Luke 3:2)?

Circle any references to baptism in the text.

LUKE 3:1–6

¹ In the fifteenth year of the reign of Tiberius Caesar, while Pontius Pilate was governor of Judea, Herod was tetrarch of Galilee, his brother Philip tetrarch of the region of Iturea and Trachonitis, and Lysanias tetrarch of Abilene, ² during the high priesthood of Annas and Caiaphas, God's word came to John the son of Zechariah in the wilderness. ³ He went into all the vicinity of the Jordan, proclaiming a baptism of repentance for the forgiveness of sins, ⁴ as it is written in the book of the words of the prophet Isaiah:

A voice of one crying out in the wilderness:

Prepare the way for the Lord;

make his paths straight!

⁵ Every valley will be filled,

and every mountain and hill will be made low;

the crooked will become straight,

the rough ways smooth,

⁶ and everyone will see the salvation of God.

LUKE 3:21–22

²¹ When all the people were baptized, Jesus also was baptized.

As he was praying, heaven opened, ²² and the Holy Spirit descended

on him in a physical appearance like a dove. And a voice came from

heaven: "You are my beloved Son; with you I am well-pleased."

Make the Christ Connection

> Read Isaiah 40:1–5 and Luke 3:1–6, 21–22.

Isaiah's message of comfort in this week's Old Testament passage set the stage for another messenger with an almost identical ministry—John the Baptist (Luke 3). John was set apart by God, even before his birth, to be a witness about Christ, the Messiah. John is the son of Elizabeth and Zechariah, relatives of Mary, the mother of Jesus.

Luke 1 tells us that an angel appeared to Zechariah while he was in the temple and told him that his son would "make ready for the Lord a prepared people" (Luke 1:17). In verse 41 of that same chapter, Luke tells us that when Mary came to visit Elizabeth, Elizabeth's baby, who would later be named John, leaped in her womb at the presence of the Christ child in Mary's womb.

> In what ways does John the Baptist's life and ministry prepare the way for Jesus?

Not only is John's ministry a fulfillment of Isaiah's prophecy, but John is also a prophet who is sent by God to deliver a difficult message. John calls people to repentance yet also carries a message of hope about the Messiah who is to come. Just as Isaiah was a messenger to God's people, John the Baptist is a messenger crying out in the wilderness, bidding those who have ears to hear to repent and prepare their hearts for the coming of the Lord. Isaiah spoke of the coming of the glory of the Lord, but John speaks of that same glory incarnate—Jesus Christ, who embodies the fullness of God's glory. Isaiah prophesied a hope that would reach all humanity, but John speaks of the Christ, who provides the hope of eternal life for people from every nation and tribe who place their faith in Jesus.

In Luke 3, John baptizes Jesus, inaugurating Christ's public ministry here on earth. As Jesus ascends from the waters of baptism, the voice of God the Father affirms Jesus as the Son of God (Luke 3:22). Because of John's ministry, all those who are there to hear John's voice hear the voice of God, who expresses His divine pleasure in His Son, Jesus.

> How does John the Baptist's ministry fulfill Isaiah's prophecy (Isaiah 40:1–5)?

Just as Isaiah was the messenger God sent to speak to Judah (Isaiah 40:3), John the Baptist is the messenger God sent to His people to prepare the way for Jesus. Isaiah told of God's intent to return and dwell with His people again (Isaiah 40:5). John the Baptist prepares the way for Jesus Christ, the Word made flesh, to dwell among us.

> How does the fulfillment of Isaiah's prophecy encourage us?
> What does it reveal about God's character?

Live it Out

Read Isaiah 40:1–5 and Luke 3:1–6, 21–22.

Our God is full of mercy. Though the people of Judah rebelled against God, bringing judgment and exile upon themselves, God did not leave them without hope. We do not have to look at our own lives for long to see the same patterns. Romans 3:23 reminds us that we have all sinned and fallen short of the glory of God. Yet, just like Judah, we are not left without hope. The people of John's day needed to be warned of God's judgment and implored to repent. And we, along with everyone around us, must be reminded that we, too, are in need of salvation.

The prophets Isaiah and John have a message that reaches us today—one that encourages us to repent and turn our hearts toward the Lord—finding our salvation in Him. God sent these prophets we read about in these passages to help us see our sin so that we might align our hearts with God's will. He used these prophets to speak both warning and hope to us. Now, however, God speaks through His Son, Jesus (Hebrews 1:1–2)—the promised Messiah whom the prophets spoke about.

Through Jesus, we have the promise of eternal life when we place our faith in Him. Christ died to save us from the punishment of sin and the eternal fate of death as sin's consequence. We can thank God for His great mercy that gives us the opportunity to respond to His message of repentance and faith. Though we will face earthly consequences for our sin, just as Judah faced exile, the promise of God's mercy to us in Christ comforts us in the same way the people of Judah were comforted. In response to God's infinite mercy and love, we can share His message of comfort with others.

Reflect on this week's verses as you answer the following questions.

How does God respond to our sin?
What is the hope we have in the midst of our sin?

How can we align our hearts with God's will? How is Jesus the answer to our sinful hearts?

Who in your life needs to hear about God's mercy and redemption? Stop and pray for that person's salvation and for the opportunity to share Christ with them.

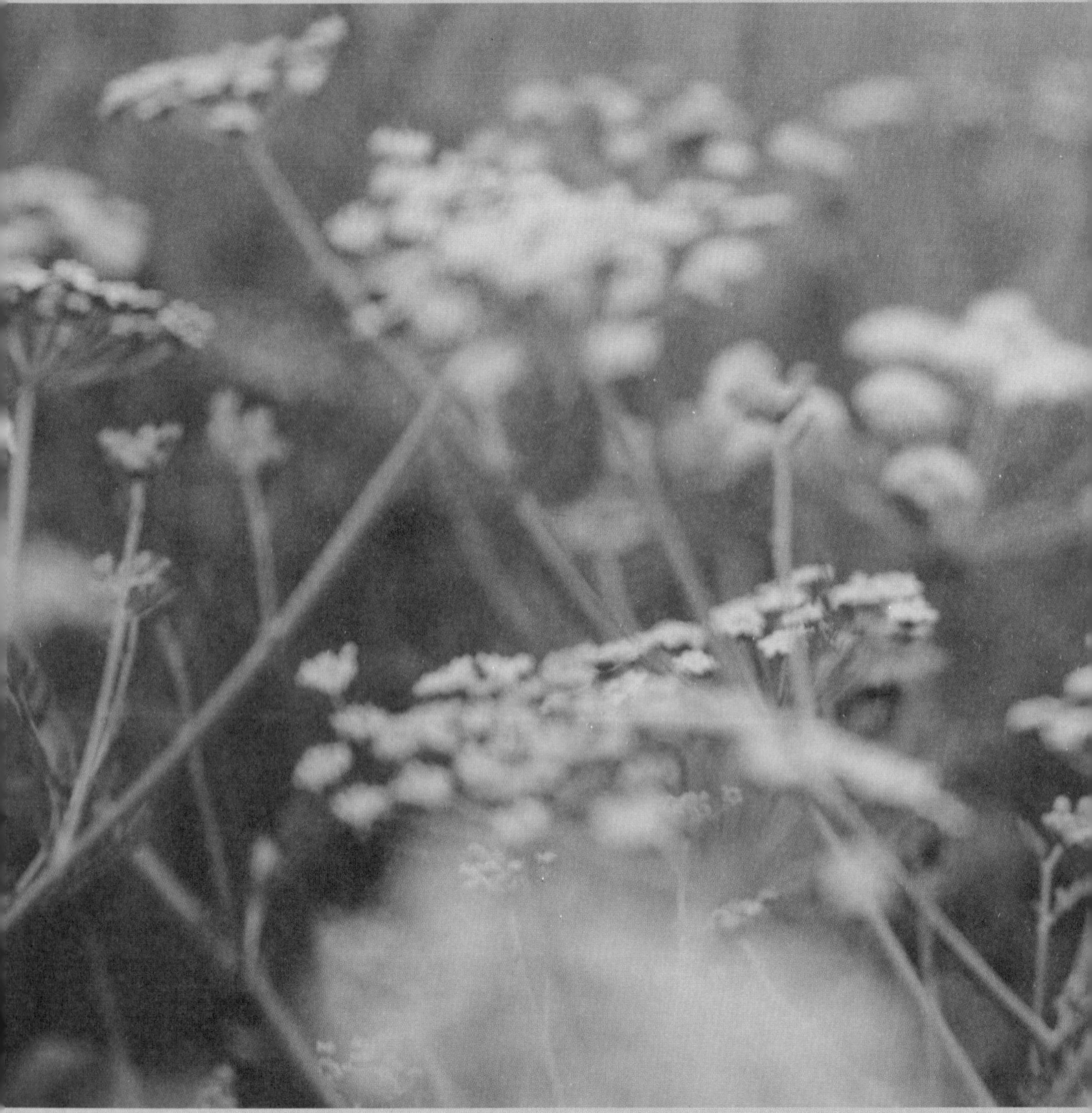

WEEK 37

Introduction

This week, we will read Isaiah 42:6–7, Isaiah 49:6, and John 8:12 and learn that Jesus is the Servant that God promised—through Isaiah—who would be a light to the nations. Through studying the themes of light and darkness, we will be encouraged to share the light of Christ with anyone we know walking in darkness today.

"It is not enough for you
to be my servant
raising up the tribes of Jacob
and restoring the protected
ones of Israel.
I will also make you a light
for the nations,
to be my salvation to the
ends of the earth."

ISAIAH 49:6

Mark it Up: Old Testament Passage

Today, we will begin studying Isaiah 42:6–7 and Isaiah 49:6. As we do, we will see God's promise to send a Servant to be a light to the nations. Read the passages multiple times and annotate, or mark up, the text as you read. For tips and examples on annotating, see pages 204–215.

Highlight any words or phrases that point to Christ.

Make note of any attributes of God seen in the text.

Circle the word "light." What or who is the light for? Who is the light?

Underline references to people or people groups (Israel, the nations, etc.).

Make note of the pronouns in these verses. Who does each one refer to?

ISAIAH 42:6-7

⁶ I am the Lord. I have called you

for a righteous purpose,

and I will hold you by your hand.

I will watch over you, and I will appoint you

to be a covenant for the people

and a light to the nations,

⁷ in order to open blind eyes,

to bring out prisoners from the dungeon,

and those sitting in darkness from the prison house.

ISAIAH 49:6

⁶ he says,

"It is not enough for you to be my servant

raising up the tribes of Jacob

and restoring the protected ones of Israel.

I will also make you a light for the nations,

to be my salvation to the ends of the earth."

Go Deeper

Read Isaiah 42:6–7 and Isaiah 49:6.

The prophecies of Isaiah are full of judgment and hope. During the time of their writing, God's people are deep in idolatry. They fail to trust God's provision and protection, and they make alliances with other nations who then lead them to worship false gods. They have turned from God and His commandments, and Isaiah prophesies about the consequences of these actions.

Read Isaiah 10:1–11. What is the judgment coming for Israel?

God is going to give Israel over to the surrounding nations—specifically the cruel and wicked nation of Assyria. They will destroy the land God has given to Israel. They will burn down the city and the homes and plunder the people. The Israelites will either be killed or taken back to Assyria, where they will be kept in captivity and exiled from their homeland. But Isaiah shows us that God's judgment is not just for Israel alone.

Read Isaiah 34:1–4. Who are the recipients of God's judgment?

While the people of Israel are God's chosen people and the ones with whom He has a covenant, it is not their disobedience alone that displeases God; the wickedness and idolatry of the nations—of all humanity—is displeasing to Him. Throughout Isaiah, judgment is proclaimed to each of the nations surrounding Israel. Then, in several places, such as Isaiah 34, God announces His anger toward all nations for their idolatry and their evil, and He promises to bring judgment to them all.

But true justice cannot come from judgment alone. In order for there to be true justice, there must also be restoration. Therefore, judgment is only half of the message of Isaiah—his message is also one of hope.

> Read Isaiah 42:1–4. How will God bring true justice to the nations?

God speaks through Isaiah and says that He will appoint a Servant whom He will strengthen and give His Spirit (Isaiah 42:1). His Servant will not grow weary and will not retreat until He has brought justice to the nations.

Isaiah 49:5 tells us that this Servant will be the Deliverer of Israel—that He will restore them and gather them back to God. But Isaiah 49:6 (as well as Isaiah 42:6–7) also tells us that this Servant will not only be a Savior of Israel but will be a light to all the nations. Through Him, all the people of the earth will be delivered from their blindness. His light will release them from darkness and bring justice to all the earth.

Mark it Up: New Testament Passage

Today, we will study John 8:12 and learn how Jesus is the Servant, promised in the book of Isaiah, who is said to be a light to the nations. Read John 8:12 multiple times and annotate, or mark up, the text as you read. For tips and examples on annotating, see pages 204–215.

Highlight any words or phrases that point to Christ.

Make note of any attributes of God seen in the text.

Circle the word "light." Who is the light, and what is it for?

Draw a box around the world "darkness."
What do you think it means to walk in darkness?

What must be done to escape darkness?
Underline where you see the answer to this question in the passage.

JOHN 8:12

¹² Jesus spoke to them again: "I am the light of the world. Anyone who follows me will never walk in the darkness but will have the light of life."

Make the Christ Connection

> Read Isaiah 42:6–7, Isaiah 49:6, and John 8:12.

The Gospel of John is incredibly rich in its theology, themes, and illustrations. One particularly interesting feature of John's Gospel is the fact that it includes seven "I Am" statements of Jesus. These are seven unique ways Jesus chooses to identify Himself and describe His mission on earth. Today, we are studying the second of these statements in which Jesus calls Himself the Light of the World.

Light and darkness are recurring themes throughout the Gospel of John. As such, John 8:12 is not the only time Jesus identifies Himself as the Light of the World. Just after this passage, we see that Jesus repeats this same phrase — "I am the light of the world" (John 8:12) — before healing a man who was born blind (John 9:6–7).

> Read John 9:1–7. How does this story connect to Isaiah 42:6–7?

Jesus was not merely performing a miracle when He restored this man's sight, and this passage is not simply referring to physical blindness. Later in John 9, Jesus makes it clear that He is speaking of spiritual blindness (John 9:35–41).

With this in mind, when we return to John 8:12, we can identify a clear connection to Isaiah 42:6–7. Jesus is the Servant who came as a light to the nations—to the world—to restore sight to the blind and deliver those in darkness. His act of healing the blind man is indeed a demonstration of His power and authority, revealing His concern for the health and well-being of His people, but it also points us to His ultimate mission of bringing justice to the earth.

> How does Jesus bring justice to the earth?

As we learned on Day 2, though Isaiah prophesied that this Servant—Jesus—would restore Israel and deliver justice, this justice was not just for Israel. God cares for all of His people, and His plan has always included the nations (Genesis 3:15, 12:2–3; Exodus 19:5–6; Isaiah 49:6). As we turn to the New Testament, we see Jesus directly identified as the Servant whom Isaiah wrote about (Luke 2:32; Acts 13:47, 26:23)—the One who comes to offer salvation to all humanity.

By taking on flesh, living faithfully, being crucified, resurrecting, and ascending to the right hand of God in order to intercede on our behalf, Christ has paid the penalty of our sins. He is faithful where we have failed, and He has delivered us from the prison of darkness (Isaiah 42:6–7), which is our sin. Now, anyone who repents and trusts in Jesus for salvation will no longer "walk in the darkness but will have the light of life" (John 8:12).

> Pray and thank God for sending Jesus to be the Servant who is the Light of the World so that we no longer have to walk in darkness.

Live it Out

> Read Isaiah 42:6–7, Isaiah 49:6, and John 8:12.

This week, we have learned that Jesus is the promised Servant from Isaiah 42 and 49. These passages tell us that Jesus came not just for Israel but for all the nations. Indeed, He is the Light of the World who has come to bring humanity out of the darkness of their sin and into His great light of life (John 8:12).

These passages, then, are extremely missional. They remind us that darkness is real, and people who do not know Jesus are trapped—or as Isaiah puts it, imprisoned—in this darkness (Isaiah 42:7). It is as if they are blind. But Jesus has come to heal those who are blind and deliver those in darkness. We are called to help bring others into the light of Christ by leading them to Jesus. May these verses compel us to pray for and share with the people in our lives who do not yet know Jesus as their Lord and Savior.

Reflect on this week's passages as you answer the following questions.

> Before Christ, describe the darkness that defined your life.

How has the light of Christ changed you?

List anyone you know who is not yet a follower of Jesus. Scripture tells us that these people who do not yet know Christ are in darkness. Pray and ask God to reveal ways you can share the light of Jesus with them. List any ways that come to mind.

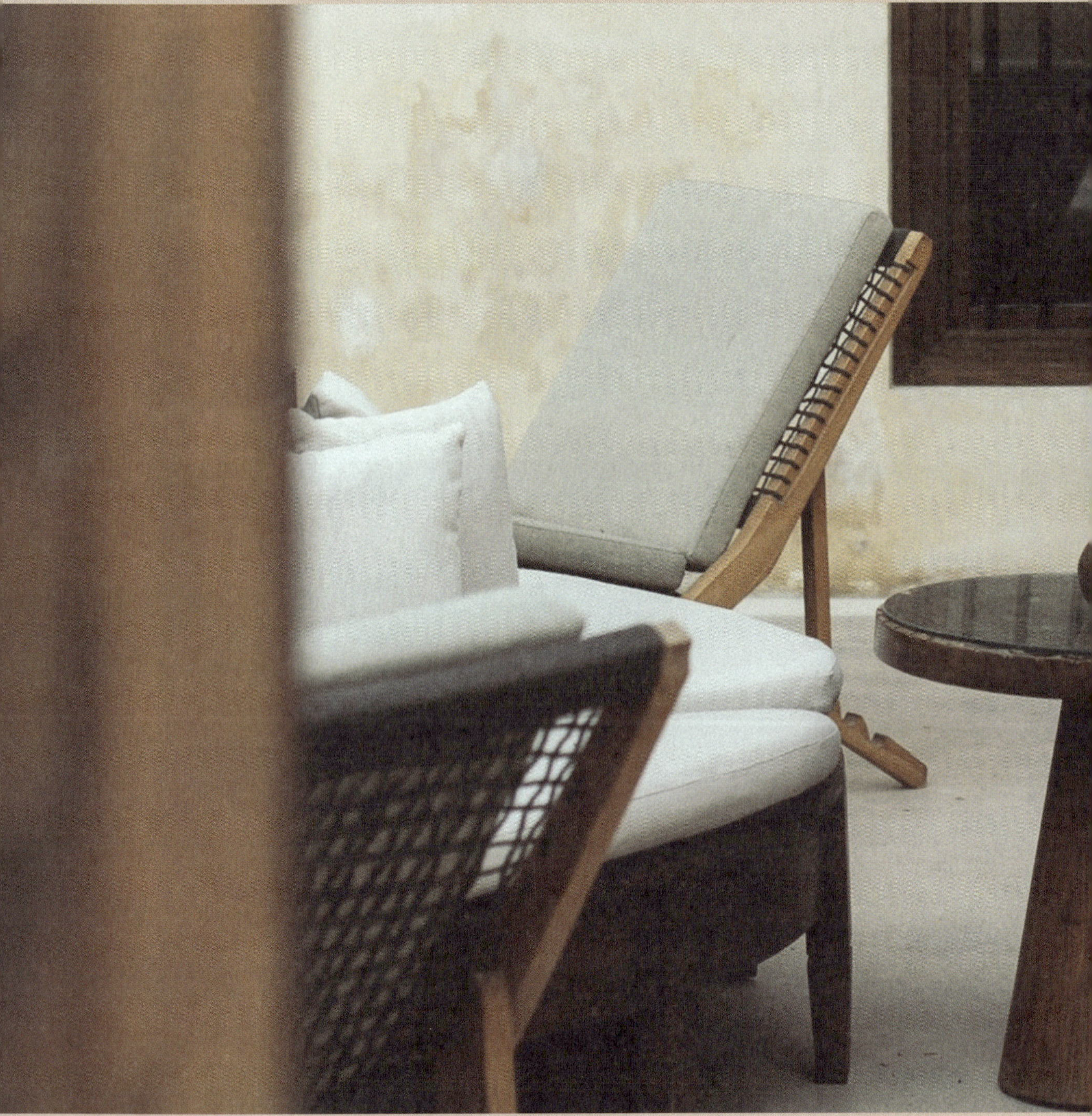

WEEK 38

Introduction

This week, we will trace themes of sacrificial service through Isaiah 52:13–53:12 and Mark 10:45, learning that Jesus is the suffering Messiah foretold by Isaiah. In response, you will be encouraged to worship Jesus as the high and exalted Lamb of God who became sin so that you could receive His righteousness. Because He so selflessly served you, may you then be encouraged to serve others.

Mark it Up: Old Testament Passage

Today, we will begin studying Isaiah's surprising description of the coming Messiah in Isaiah 52:13–53:12. Isaiah foretells a Messiah who knows rejection and suffering, and his prophecy points to Jesus, who would come not to be served but to serve His people. Read the passage two or three times and annotate, or mark up, the text as you read. For tips and examples on annotating, see pages 204–215.

Highlight any words or phrases that point to Christ.

Make note of any attributes of God seen in the text.

Break this text up into smaller chunks to help you understand the passage. To do so, draw a line between verses. Do this by observing natural breaks in the text, by looking at conjunctions (words like *for, and, nor, but, or, yet, so*), etc. *(Hint: there is no right or wrong way to do this!)* What does this exercise teach you?

Highlight in a different color any descriptions of the suffering servant in this passage. What does this teach you about the coming Messiah?

Underline any references to the results of the Messiah's service. How does this help you understand what Christ accomplished?

ISAIAH 52:13–15

[13] See, my servant will be successful;

he will be raised and lifted up and greatly exalted.

[14] Just as many were appalled at you—

his appearance was so disfigured

that he did not look like a man,

and his form did not resemble a human being—

[15] so he will sprinkle many nations.

Kings will shut their mouths because of him,

for they will see what had not been told them,

and they will understand what they had not heard.

ISAIAH 53:1–12

¹ Who has believed what we have heard?

And to whom has the arm of the Lord been revealed?

² He grew up before him like a young plant

and like a root out of dry ground.

He didn't have an impressive form

or majesty that we should look at him,

no appearance that we should desire him.

³ He was despised and rejected by men,

a man of suffering who knew what sickness was.

He was like someone people turned away from;

he was despised, and we didn't value him.

⁴ Yet he himself bore our sicknesses,

and he carried our pains;

but we in turn regarded him stricken,

struck down by God, and afflicted.

⁵ But he was pierced because of our rebellion,

crushed because of our iniquities;

punishment for our peace was on him,

and we are healed by his wounds.

⁶ We all went astray like sheep;

we all have turned to our own way;

and the Lord has punished him

for the iniquity of us all.

⁷ He was oppressed and afflicted,

yet he did not open his mouth.

Like a lamb led to the slaughter

and like a sheep silent before her shearers,

he did not open his mouth.

⁸ He was taken away because of oppression and judgment,

and who considered his fate?

For he was cut off from the land of the living;

he was struck because of my people's rebellion.

⁹ He was assigned a grave with the wicked,

but he was with a rich man at his death,

because he had done no violence

and had not spoken deceitfully.

¹⁰ Yet the Lord was pleased to crush him severely.

When you make him a guilt offering,

he will see his seed, he will prolong his days,

and by his hand, the Lord's pleasure will be accomplished.

¹¹ After his anguish,

he will see light and be satisfied.

By his knowledge,

my righteous servant will justify many,

and he will carry their iniquities.

¹² Therefore I will give him the many as a portion,

and he will receive the mighty as spoil,

because he willingly submitted to death,

and was counted among the rebels;

yet he bore the sin of many

and interceded for the rebels.

Go Deeper

> Read Isaiah 52:13–53:12.

As we have previously discussed, Isaiah 52:13–53:12 is the fourth of Isaiah's "Servant Songs" (see "Extra: The Servant Songs of Isaiah" on page 186). These songs speak of a Servant who will come to rescue God's people. However, Isaiah's Servant Songs make it clear that this rescue will not come as the people might expect. Their rescue — their salvation — will come through a suffering Servant, a servant who is described in great detail in Isaiah 52:13–53:12.

> Read Isaiah 53:1–9. What are some descriptors of the coming Messiah?

Isaiah's prophecy of the coming Messiah does not sound like a modern depiction of a hero. He does not wear a cape, nor is He handsome. He does not come in shining armor or command a fearsome army. Instead, He is rejected by men, despised, and unvalued. He does not boast a majestic form. He is like a sheep led to the slaughter.

Though He is not violent and does not speak deceitfully, the Messiah bears the punishment of iniquity for us all. Isaiah prophesies that the Messiah will be pierced for our rebellion and crushed for our iniquities. By His wounds, God's people will be healed.

Why is this kind of Messiah necessary? Why do we read such a surprisingly sad depiction of the One who comes to save?

> Read Leviticus 19:1–2. In this passage, what does God command His people to do?

In Leviticus, God commanded His people to be holy because He is holy. God made His people image-bearers — able to be kind, to solve problems, and to create. God wanted His people to bear His image in holiness. However, sin disrupted Israel's ability to obey God's law. Instead, God's people rebelled against Him. Like sheep, they went astray and turned to their own way (Isaiah 53:6).

This sin created a chasm between God and His people. The Israelites were unholy people loved by a holy God. And so, in order to be in a relationship with His people, God created a sacrificial system to atone for the sins of His people.

> Read Leviticus 17:11. Through what does atonement for sin come?

Sin has a cost, and in God's perfection, He deemed that the cost of sin must be blood. Therefore, on the annual Day of Atonement (which is described in detail in Leviticus 16), the Israelites would make several ritual sacrifices to atone for their sins. With this payment of blood, God could dwell among His people in the tabernacle. As God's people tried to go astray, God created a system in which He could dwell near.

And He would do this eternally through the Messiah. As Isaiah prophesied, the Messiah would be pierced for our transgressions so that God could dwell with His people once and for all (Isaiah 53:5). The Messiah would be cut off from the land of the living so that God's people never would be (Isaiah 53:8). The Messiah faced judgment so that God's people would never face eternal judgment (Isaiah 53:8).

> Read Isaiah 52:13–15 and Isaiah 53:10–12.
> What are the results of the Messiah's sacrifice?

The Messiah, who would give His life for many as we will see in the New Testament, would not be lowly forever. He would come to accomplish God's good will. After the Messiah experiences anguish, He will see the light. God's Servant will be successful and highly exalted. Because the Messiah willingly gives His life, God's people will become His own.

Mark it Up: New Testament Passage

Today, you will read Mark 10:45 and learn that Jesus is the suffering Savior foretold in Isaiah 52:13–53:12. Read Mark 10:45 multiple times and annotate, or mark up, the text as you read. For tips and examples on annotating, see pages 204–215.

Highlight any words or phrases that point to Christ.

Make note of any attributes of God seen in the text.

Circle "the Son of Man." Who is this referring to?

Underline why the Son of Man did *not* come. Now, double-underline why He *did* come. Why do you think the author of the Gospel of Mark chose to distinguish why the Messiah came in this way?

Highlight in a different color how the Messiah serves. How does this remind you of Isaiah 52:13–53:12?

MARK 10:45

[45] For even the Son of Man did not come to be served,

but to serve, and to give his life as a ransom for many.

Make the Christ Connection

> Read Isaiah 52:13–53:12 and Mark 10:45.

Isaiah's prophecy of the coming Messiah is counterintuitive to how we might imagine a Savior. This Savior would be a man who suffered—a man who was oppressed and afflicted. But not only would He suffer, He would suffer for God's people. This man would be pierced for the people's rebellion, crushed for their iniquities, and punished for their peace. Even more, this Messiah would be punished by God, and this punishment would please God. Why? Because this righteous Servant would justify many and intercede for those who rebelled against Him. This is not a hero that man would dream up; this is a story of redemption authored by God alone—a story in which God's perfect Son would die for the sins of His people.

> Read Mark 10:35–45. How does the request of James and John reveal the desires of their hearts? How does this contrast to Jesus's role as a servant?

Jesus is the Savior—the humble Lamb of God who comes to serve rather than to be served. But in Mark 10:35–45, we see a stark contrast between Jesus's priorities and those of James and John. While Isaiah 52:13–53:12 depicted Jesus's role as a suffering Servant—selfless and humble—James and John ask to sit at Jesus's right and left in glory. While Jesus lowers Himself to serve humanity, James and John wish to be elevated.

In this context, Jesus teaches a divine truth about Himself that His followers must imitate: in order to be great, one must be a servant, and in order to be first, one must be a slave to all (Mark 10:43–44). Jesus teaches us that godly righteousness will never be self-righteous. Rather, godly righteousness serves, and Jesus commands His disciples—and us today—to serve in His footsteps.

Read Hebrews 12:2. What is the joy set before Jesus?
(Hint: think about Isaiah 53:11–12.)

Jesus's suffering was never in vain. He experienced mocking, beating, betrayal, and crucifixion for the greater joy that lay before Him—to bear the sin of many and intercede on behalf of rebels (Isaiah 53:12). The joy set before Jesus was to see God's people redeemed, brought into a right relationship with the Father, and welcomed into heaven.

From a human point of view, Jesus died a shameful criminal's death on the cross. But God's wisdom far surpasses human wisdom. His suffering was temporary, for Jesus rose again in glory and was seated at the right hand of the Father. God used this criminal's death to give life to many—to pay the ransom for sin and adopt sons and daughters as His own. Jesus became like a Lamb led to the slaughter so that His people's crimson-red sins may be white like wool. This is the joy set before Jesus—to relinquish God's people from the shackles of sin and usher them into eternal joy. This is the life of a suffering servant.

Reread Mark 10:45. Take a moment to rest in this truth. Thank God for sending His Son, Jesus, as our suffering Servant so that we may be called children of God.

Live it Out

> Read Isaiah 52:13–53:12 and Mark 10:45.

This week, we have learned that Jesus is the suffering Servant foretold by the prophet Isaiah. He was like a lamb led to the slaughter (Isaiah 53:7); He was the God-man who committed no crime yet died a criminal's death. Jesus committed no violence, yet He was cut off from the land of the living (Isaiah 53:8–9). He was the long-awaited Messiah who was treated like an enemy. In Jesus was the fullness of God, yet He emptied Himself by assuming the form of a servant, taking on the likeness of humanity. He humbled Himself by becoming obedient to the point of death—even death on a cross (Philippians 2:7–8).

As Jesus teaches in Mark 10:35–45, those who want to be with Him in glory must follow in His footsteps. In other words, whoever wants to become great must become a servant, considering others as more important than themselves (Philippians 2:3). Jesus's example changes our relationships, for no longer do we expect others to serve us, but we serve others as Jesus served us. No longer do we show kindness to receive kindness in return, but we show kindness because Jesus has shown us kindness. No longer do we forgive so that we may be forgiven, but we forgive because we have already been forgiven in Christ.

Jesus has set a standard for us. Today, behold the suffering Servant who gave His life so that we may have life—who bore the punishment for each of our sins for the pleasure of seeing us reconciled to the Father. May His obedience lead you to worship Him—the King who came to serve. May you follow in Jesus's footsteps and live, not to be exalted on earth but to be exalted in heaven.

Reflect on this week's passages as you answer the following questions.

> Do you find it difficult to consider others as more important than yourself? Why?

How does Jesus's servant heart inspire you to serve others?

Consider what an eternity with Jesus will be like. How does knowing your treasure in heaven inspire you to serve others as Jesus served?

The Servant Songs of Isaiah

Throughout Isaiah 41–55, references are often made to God's "servant." In some instances (especially in chapters 41–48), this refers to the nation of Israel, which was meant to represent God before the world but instead was blind and deaf (Isaiah 42:18–20). But in the other instances, the "servant" refers to a specific individual who is faithful to God and represents Him to the nations.

Four passages — often referred to as Isaiah's "Servant Songs" — describe this second servant: Isaiah 42:1–9, Isaiah 49:1–7, Isaiah 50:4–9, and Isaiah 52:13–53:12. Many of the details found in these passages are picked up in the New Testament and applied to Jesus. The following are excerpts taken from each of Isaiah's four Servant Songs:

> This is my servant; I strengthen him,
> this is my chosen one; I delight in him.
> I have put my Spirit on him;
> he will bring justice to the nations.
>
> **ISAIAH 42:1**

> he says,
> "It is not enough for you to be my servant
> raising up the tribes of Jacob
> and restoring the protected ones of Israel.
> I will also make you a light for the nations,
> to be my salvation to the ends of the earth."
>
> **ISAIAH 49:6**

> The Lord GOD has given me
> the tongue of those who are instructed
> to know how to sustain the weary with a word.
> He awakens me each morning;
> he awakens my ear to listen like those being instructed.
>
> **ISAIAH 50:4**

> But he was pierced because of our rebellion,
> crushed because of our iniquities;
> punishment for our peace was on him,
> and we are healed by his wounds.
> We all went astray like sheep;
> we all have turned to our own way;
> and the LORD has punished him
> for the iniquity of us all.
>
> **ISAIAH 53:5–6**

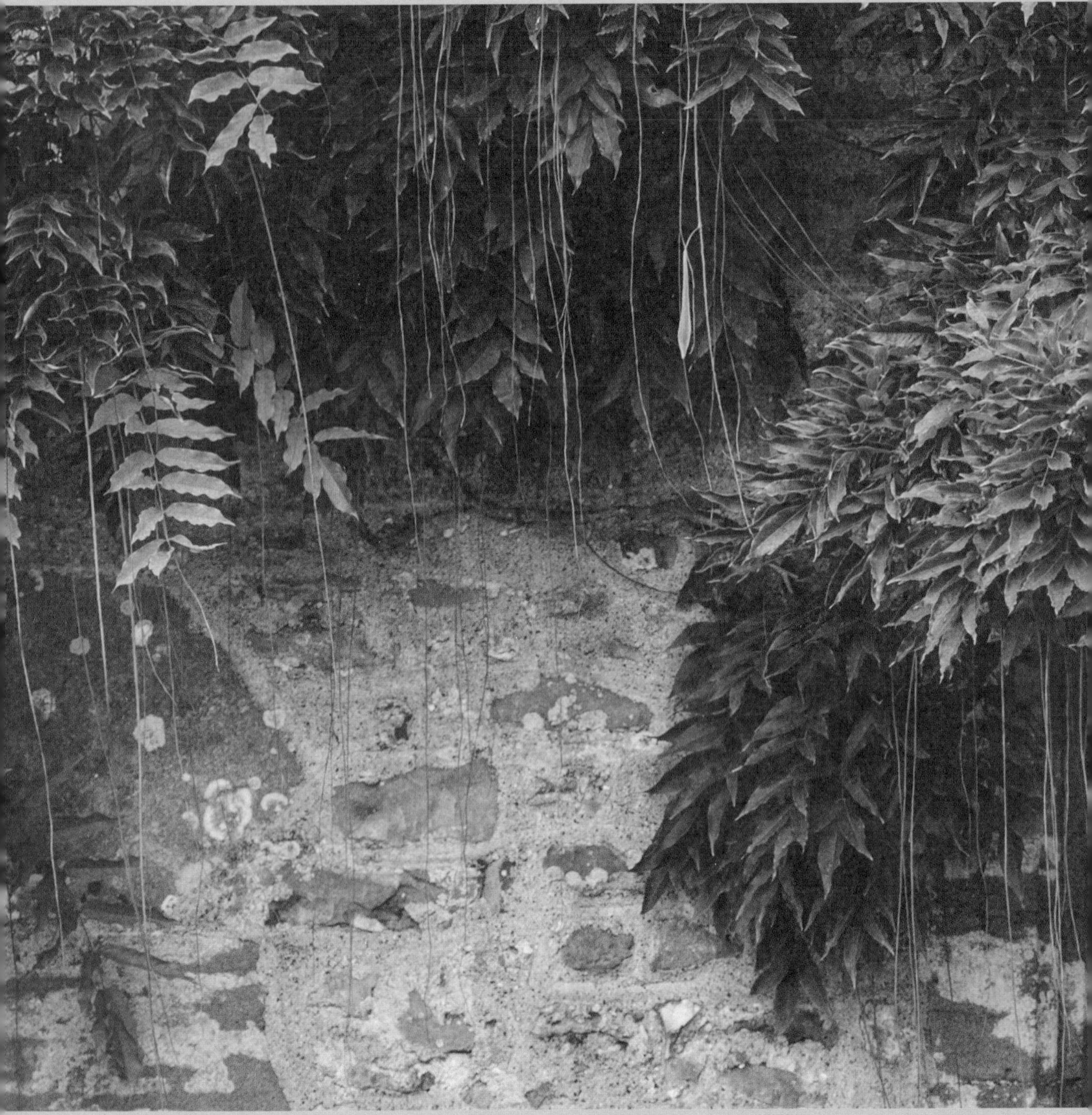

WEEK 39

Introduction

This week, we will look at Jeremiah's prophecy of a new covenant (Jeremiah 31:31–34) and how Jesus references this prophecy in His last meal with the disciples before His crucifixion (Luke 22:14–20). In these passages, we will see that Jesus's death is the means through which God enacts this new covenant in which He forgives our sins and enables us to walk in His ways.

Mark it Up: Old Testament Passage

Today, we will begin our study by looking at Jeremiah 31:31–34 and exploring the kind of covenant that God promises to one day make. Read the passage multiple times and annotate, or mark up, the text as you read. For tips and examples on annotating, see pages 204–215.

> Highlight any words or phrases that point to Christ.

> Make note of any attributes of God seen in the text.

> Circle any descriptions of what this covenant *will* be like.

> Underline any descriptions of what this covenant *will not* be like.

> Draw a line out to the margin and write out the two covenants that are being contrasted.

> Read verse 32. Highlight in another color the reason that God gives for making a new covenant. Why was a new covenant needed?

JEREMIAH 31:31-34

³¹ "Look, the days are coming"—this is the LORD's declaration—"when I will make a new covenant with the house of Israel and with the house of Judah.

³² This one will not be like the covenant I made with their ancestors on the day I took them by the hand to lead them out of the land of Egypt—my covenant that they broke even though I am their master"—the LORD's declaration.

³³ "Instead, this is the covenant I will make with the house of Israel after those days"—the LORD's declaration. "I will put my teaching within them and write it on their hearts. I will be their God, and they will be my people. ³⁴ No longer will one teach his neighbor or his brother, saying, 'Know the LORD,' for they will all know me, from the least to the greatest of them"—this is the LORD's declaration. "For I will forgive their iniquity and never again remember their sin."

Go Deeper

> Read Jeremiah 31:31–34.

When God rescued the Israelites from Egypt, He brought them to Mount Sinai and entered into a covenant relationship with them. Many of this covenant's requirements are listed in Exodus 20–23, chapters that describe how Israel was to live in the Promised Land. The Israelites responded to these commands by declaring that they would obey everything God had required of them (Exodus 24:3, 7). With this declaration and with the shedding of "the blood of the covenant," God and Israel officially entered into a covenant (Exodus 24:8).

But Israel's confident declaration in Exodus 24 feels a little ironic in retrospect. Just a few chapters later, in Exodus 32, they rebelled against God by constructing a golden calf. And they continued to rebel in the centuries that followed. In Deuteronomy 27–28, God warned Israel of judgments to come if they turned from Him, including being exiled from the land. Sure enough, centuries after God first gave these warnings, the prophet Jeremiah would find himself on the cusp of their fulfillment.

> Read Jeremiah 1:4–8. What task does God give Jeremiah to do?
> How does Jeremiah 1:17–19 underscore the difficulty of this task?

Jeremiah had a very difficult life. He lived during the final days of the southern kingdom of Judah and endured Babylon's brutal siege and destruction of Jerusalem, along with its aftermath. On top of this was the difficult task of delivering God's message of judgment to Judah and making some powerful enemies in the process (Jeremiah 1:18–19). Jeremiah was tasked with telling the people of Judah that they had broken the covenant (Jeremiah 11:1–17), that they should submit to Babylon (Jeremiah 27:1–15), and that their exile in Babylon would be long, not short (Jeremiah 25:1–14, 28:1–4, 29:4–9). Needless to say, he was likely not popular with the people of Judah.

But though God had warned His people of exile in the book of Deuteronomy, He also pointed to hope for a glorious future. And Jeremiah reflects this same hope.

> Read Deuteronomy 4:25–31 and Jeremiah 29:10–14.
> What parallels do you see between these passages?

God promises that if His people seek Him with all of their hearts, they will find Him, and He will restore them to the Promised Land. Yet their centuries of chronic disobedience does not exactly inspire hope that they will automatically be different once they return to their land.

But God has a solution for that: He promises to make a new covenant with His people (Jeremiah 31:31–34). This covenant will be different from the one they failed to keep. In this new covenant, God will write His laws on His people's hearts, causing them to walk in His ways. And He will forgive their sins. In perhaps the bleakest moment of Israel's history, God promises that a glorious future still awaits them.

> Have you, like the Israelites, found obeying God to be easier said than done? What comfort can you take from the new covenant mentioned in this passage?

Mark it Up: New Testament Passage

After spending time in Jeremiah 31:31–34, we will now shift our focus to Luke 22:14–20 to dwell on its connection to Jeremiah. Read the passage multiple times and annotate, or mark up, the text as you read. For tips and examples on annotating, see pages 204–215.

> Highlight any words or phrases that point to Christ.

> Make note of any attributes of God seen in the text.

> Circle any words in this passage that reflect language from Jeremiah 31.

> Underline the meanings Jesus gives to the bread and the cup.

> Highlight in another color the name Jesus gives to this meal in verse 15. What do you think is the significance of this word in the Bible?

LUKE 22:14-20

¹⁴ When the hour came, he reclined at the table, and the apostles with him.

¹⁵ Then he said to them, "I have fervently desired to eat this Passover with you before I suffer. ¹⁶ For I tell you, I will not eat it again until it is fulfilled in the kingdom of God." ¹⁷ Then he took a cup, and after giving thanks, he said, "Take this and share it among yourselves. ¹⁸ For I tell you, from now on I will not drink of the fruit of the vine until the kingdom of God comes."

¹⁹ And he took bread, gave thanks, broke it, gave it to them, and said, "This is my body, which is given for you. Do this in remembrance of me."

²⁰ In the same way he also took the cup after supper and said, "This cup is the new covenant in my blood, which is poured out for you."

Make the Christ Connection

> Read Luke 22:1–23.

Luke 22 records one of the more well-known moments of Jesus's life: the final meal He shared with His disciples before His death, a meal often referred to as the Last Supper. But what is sometimes overlooked is that Jesus is celebrating not just any meal but the Passover meal with His disciples—something Luke repeatedly mentions (Luke 22:1, 7, 8, 11, 13, 15).

God had instituted this annual meal as a way for Israel to commemorate their deliverance from slavery in Egypt (Exodus 12–14). During this meal, they would pass around four cups of wine, eat unleavened bread and a lamb, retell the Exodus story, and sing the words of Psalms 113–118.

> Why do you think God had Israel observe the Passover meal each year?

In the midst of this meal that commemorated God's salvation of Israel from slavery, Jesus takes the bread and one of the cups of wine and re-centers their meaning around Himself. He tells His disciples that the bread signifies His body "given for you," which they are to now eat in commemoration of Him (Luke 22:19). And the wine signifies His blood, "poured out for you" (Luke 22:20). Jesus is speaking of His death—a particularly violent one at that. And the words "for you" indicate that He will die in the place of others.

But what Jesus says about the wine in particular is significant. He calls it "the new covenant in my blood." Just as God's covenant with Israel had been ratified by "the blood of the covenant" (Exodus 24:8), so now will Jesus's blood ratify a covenant—specifically, the new covenant spoken of in Jeremiah 31:31–34.

> Looking back at Jeremiah 31:31–34, what had God promised to do in the new covenant? How does Jesus's death accomplish this?

One of the benefits of the new covenant promised in Jeremiah 31 included the forgiveness of sins. And as Jesus mentions in this scene, His death will be "for"—that is, in place of—"you." In His death, He would take the full punishment that sin deserves, His death on the cross paving the way for sinners to be forgiven and reconciled to God.

Another benefit was that God would write His law on the hearts of His people, causing them to walk in His ways. Or, as Ezekiel described it, God would remove their heart of stone, give them a heart of flesh, and place His Spirit within them (Ezekiel 36:26–27). Jesus would also accomplish this by ascending into heaven and sending the Holy Spirit to all He has saved (Acts 2:32–33, Romans 8:1–4).

Because of Jesus's death in our place, our sins are forgiven, and we are enabled to love and obey God, with whom we now have a covenant relationship.

> Spend time praising God for the benefits of the new covenant and for sending Jesus to bring us into a relationship with Himself.

Live it Out

> Read Jeremiah 31:31–34 and Luke 22:14–20.

When reading the Old Testament, it can be easy for us to judge the Israelites. We might smirk at their confident declaration in Exodus 24:3–7 that they will obey everything God commanded them, knowing that they will do no such thing (Jeremiah 11:7–8).

But if we are being honest with ourselves, we are not so different. We make declarations and grand plans of living in obedience to God's commands, only to find that actually living such a life is quite difficult. We need more than simply knowing what God's commands are; we need the desire to obey them. And that is precisely what God provides for us through the new covenant inaugurated by Christ, along with the forgiveness of our sins (Jeremiah 31:33–34).

Reflect on this week's verses as you answer the following questions.

> How do you typically respond when you have sinned against God? Do you ever find yourself unwilling to approach Him in prayer out of a sense of guilt? How can the new covenant comfort you in these moments?

In what ways have you seen your desire to obey God grow throughout your life as a Christian? Spend time thanking God for this.

How can the passages we have looked at this week enhance your appreciation of the Lord's Supper? What are we calling to mind when we partake of it?

Volume 3 Conclusion

Congratulations! If you have reached this page, that means you are now three-quarters of the way through the *Christ in All of Scripture* study set. In this third volume, you have read, annotated, and considered many passages from across the Old and New Testaments. And in doing so, you have continued to see how all of Scripture points us to Jesus Christ.

We began this volume in Ezra, where God's people rebuilt the tabernacle after the destruction of Jerusalem. We then spent several weeks in the Psalms and Isaiah, and finally, we ended in the book of Jeremiah. Throughout, we have seen how Jesus is the hope for God's people and the center of what God is doing in the world.

But there is still one more volume to go. As the pages of the Bible continue to unfold, there are many more exciting Christ connections to be made! So, we invite you to continue your study with us in *Christ in All of Scripture | Volume 4*, which begins by looking at how the prophet Ezekiel points to Jesus as the Good Shepherd and continues on to consider how Christ is seen in the rest of the prophets. Finally, our fourth and final volume will conclude by inviting you to return to the first pages of the Bible and consider them in light of Christ's final restoration of all things.

As we continue to study God's Word, may we continually grow in our love for Him. May we rejoice in His glorious plan of redemption, which is on display from the first pages of Genesis to the final chapters of Revelation. And may we ultimately worship Christ for all He has done on our behalf. He is the main character of the story. And so, let us continue to commit ourselves to seeing His fingerprints on every page.

You can find Christ in All of Scripture | Volume 4—*along with each of the other volumes and many more resources to equip you in your study of God's Word—at www.thedailygraceco.com.*

We need more than simply knowing
what God's commands are;
we need the desire to obey them.

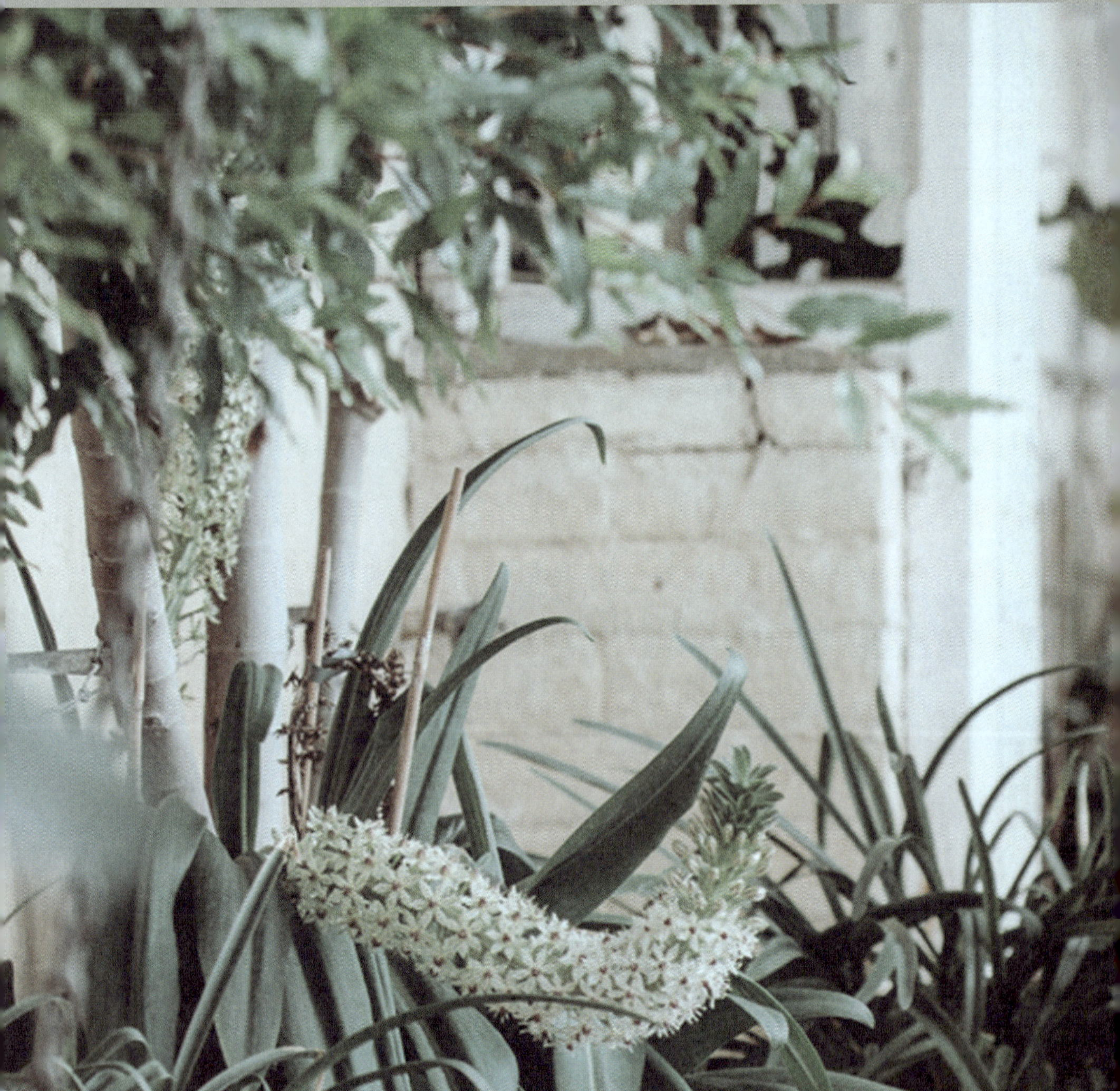

Appendix

The content in this Appendix is adapted from Week 1: Prep Week from the first volume of this study. To access the full Prep Week content—complete with more examples and illustrations—check out *Christ in All of Scripture | Volume 1*, available at www.thedailygraceco.com, or scan the QR code below.

APPENDIX A

How to See Christ in All of Scripture

The study you hold in your hands centers on how we can find Christ in all of Scripture. But practically, how can we do so? The following chart describes seven elements you can look for in each passage—along with examples from the story of Noah in Genesis 6–9—that will point you in the right direction as you journey through Scripture. You may not find each of these elements in every passage you study, but often, one or more will be present, pointing you to Jesus Christ—even in the most unexpected places.

WHAT TO LOOK FOR	EXAMPLE (FROM GENESIS 6–9)
Roles: Positions seen throughout Scripture that are filled perfectly by Christ	There are many roles in the Old Testament that find their fulfillment in Christ. We can see this specifically in the roles of prophets, priests, and kings—three roles which Jesus perfectly fulfilled through His life, death, resurrection, and ascension into heaven. But there are more than just these. For example, Noah plays the role of a leader in Genesis 6–9 as he leads his family to salvation through the ark, just as Christ leads His people to salvation through His death and resurrection.
Problems: Examples of sin, brokenness, hurt, failure, or any other problems that are solved only through Christ	*See Genesis 6:5.* The human heart is evil, and wickedness fills the earth. This problem can only be solved through Christ, who is able to transform the hearts of humanity.
Symbols: Images or actions that predict an aspect of Christ's person or work	*See Genesis 7:23.* Only those who entered the ark were saved from God's judgment, just like only those who are in Christ will be saved from eternal judgment.

WHAT TO LOOK FOR	EXAMPLE (FROM GENESIS 6–9)
Themes: Concepts that repeat throughout Scripture and find their resolution in Christ	*See Genesis 9:1–7.* In these verses, God makes a covenant with Noah and his family that resembles the covenant made with Adam and Eve in Genesis 1:28–30. Covenants—or God's promises to His people—are a theme throughout Scripture. Through Christ, God's new covenant is established; therefore, this theme is ultimately resolved through Him.
Promises: Specific words of God that offer assurance of His faithfulness and are fulfilled in Christ	*See Genesis 9:15–16.* God promises to remember His covenant with Noah and not destroy humanity again. This promise finds its fulfillment in the coming of Christ, who makes a way for humanity to be saved and redeemed.
People: Figures throughout Scripture who point to Christ—sometimes through their success and faithfulness but, more often, through their failure to live up to their calling, thus pointing to Christ's perfection	*See Genesis 6:9 and 9:18–27.* Noah was righteous, found favor with God, and walked with Him, and God used Noah to save his family. But Noah was not perfect, as evidenced by his sin after the flood in Genesis 9:18–27. Noah could not change his own heart or the hearts of the people. This points to humanity's need for a Savior. Thankfully, Jesus is a true and better Noah. He is able to deliver people from judgment and transform their hearts.
Predictions: Passages that speak about future events that find their ultimate fulfillment in Christ	Such predictions are found mostly in the prophetic books of the Old Testament, so there is not an example from Genesis 6–9. *Examples include: Isaiah 9:6, Hosea 1:11.*

APPENDIX B

The Attributes of God

Another way we can see Christ in all of Scripture is by identifying and studying the attributes of God. These are the traits that are true of God throughout all time and history. And because our God is a triune God—three in one—these attributes are true of all three members of the Trinity: Father, Son, and Holy Spirit. As you work through this study, you may find it helpful to bookmark this page and come back to it often as you seek to discover glimpses and echoes of Christ's character and work in every passage you study.

Eternal

God has no beginning and no end. He always was, always is, and always will be.

HAB. 1:12 / REV. 1:8 / ISA. 41:4

Faithful

God is incapable of anything but fidelity. He is loyally devoted to His plan and purpose.

2 TIM. 2:13 / DEUT. 7:9 / HEB. 10:23

Good

God is pure; there is no defilement in Him. He is unable to sin, and all He does is good.

GEN. 1:31 / PS. 34:8 / PS. 107:1

Gracious

God is kind, giving us gifts and benefits we do not deserve.

2 KINGS 13:23 / PS. 145:8 / ISA. 30:18

Holy

God is undefiled and unable to be in the presence of defilement. He is sacred and set-apart.

REV. 4:8 / LEV. 19:2 / HAB. 1:13

Incomprehensible

God is high above and beyond human understanding. He is unable to be fully known.

PS. 145:3 / ISA. 55:8-9 / ROM. 11:33-36

Immutable

God does not change. He is the same yesterday, today, and tomorrow.

1 SAM. 15:29 / ROM. 11:29 / JAMES 1:17

Infinite

God is limitless. He exhibits all of His attributes perfectly and boundlessly.

ROM. 11:33-36 / ISA. 40:28 / PS. 147:5

Jealous

God is desirous of receiving the praise and affection He rightly deserves.

EXOD. 20:5 / DEUT. 4:23-24 / JOSH. 24:19

Just

God governs in perfect justice. He acts in accordance with justice. In Him, there is no wrongdoing or dishonesty.

ISA. 61:8 / DEUT. 32:4 / PS. 146:7-9

Loving

God is eternally, enduringly, steadfastly loving and affectionate. He does not forsake or betray His covenant love.

JOHN 3:16 / EPH. 2:4-5 / 1 JOHN 4:16

Merciful

God is compassionate, withholding from us the wrath that we deserve.

TITUS 3:5 / PS. 25:10 / LAM. 3:22-23

Omnipotent

God is all-powerful; His strength is unlimited.

MATT. 19:26 / JOB 42:1-2 / JER. 32:27

Omnipresent

God is everywhere; His presence is near and permeating.

PROV. 15:3 / PS. 139:7-10 / JER. 23:23-24

Omniscient

God is all-knowing; there is nothing unknown to Him.

PS. 147:4 / 1 JOHN 3:20 / HEB. 4:13

Patient

God is long-suffering and enduring. He gives ample opportunity for people to turn toward Him.

ROM. 2:4 / 2 PET. 3:9 / PS. 86:15

Self-Existent

God was not created but exists by His power alone.

PS. 90:1-2 / JOHN 1:4 / JOHN 5:26

Self-Sufficient

God has no needs and depends on nothing, but everything depends on God.

ISA. 40:28-31 / ACTS 17:24-25 / PHIL. 4:19

Sovereign

God governs over all things; He is in complete control.

COL. 1:17 / PS. 24:1-2 / 1 CHRON. 29:11-12

Truthful

God is our measurement of what is fact. By Him we are able to discern true and false.

JOHN 3:33 / ROM. 1:25 / JOHN 14:6

Wise

God is infinitely knowledgeable and is judicious with His knowledge.

ISA. 46:9-10 / ISA. 55:9 / PROV. 3:19

Wrathful

God stands in opposition to all that is evil. He enacts judgment according to His holiness, righteousness, and justice.

PS. 69:24 / JOHN 3:36 / ROM. 1:18

As you begin annotating, remember that we do not expect you to annotate every passage perfectly.

APPENDIX C

Annotation Examples and Tips

Each week of this study provides you with the opportunity to annotate two passages of Scripture — one from the Old Testament and one from the New Testament. In doing so, you will grow in your ability to study Scripture and make Christ connections in each passage you encounter. However, if the idea of annotation seems intimidating to you, do not fret! We have provided some helpful examples on the following pages, showing you what this might look like in a few different passages of Scripture.

As you begin annotating, remember that we do not expect you to annotate every passage perfectly. Additionally, if you come across an annotation prompt that challenges you or leaves you with more questions than answers, that's okay! You may find it helpful to look at the surrounding context of that passage (i.e., the verses or chapters that come just before and just after it). And at times, you may simply jot down your questions to come back to later in the week.

TIPS FOR ANNOTATING A PASSAGE

1. Look up key words in a concordance to identify cross-references.

2. Read the surrounding context of the passage (i.e., the verses or chapters that come before or after it) to aid your understanding.

3. As you look for connections to Jesus, use highlighters and/or write notes and questions in the margins.

4. If it is difficult to see the connection to Jesus, that's okay! Pray, read the verses surrounding the passage, and be patient as you read. Each week, the commentary will help you make those connections.

5. In addition to making notes in the margins, there will be space for you to jot down notes underneath each annotation prompt. If you don't have notes, feel free to leave those spaces blank!

EXAMPLE ANNOTATION 1

PSALM 23

The Good Shepherd

A psalm of David.

¹ The (LORD) is my shepherd; *provider / protector*

I have what I need.

² (He) lets me lie down in green pastures;

(he) leads me beside quiet waters.

³ (He) renews my life; *merciful*

sovereign (he) leads me along the right paths

for (his) name's sake.

⁴ Even when I go through the darkest valley,

I fear no danger,

Circle the words that describe God or are from God.
Underline the actions of God.
Make note of where you see His attributes.

for you are with me;   *loving*

your rod and your staff—they comfort me.

⁵ You prepare a table before me   *gracious*

in the presence of my enemies;

you anoint my head with oil;

my cup overflows.

good   ⁶ Only goodness and faithful love will pursue me   *faithful*

all the days of my life,

and I will dwell in the house of the LORD   *omnipresent*

as long as I live.

EXAMPLE ANNOTATION 2

PSALM 2

Coronation of the Son

Problem (rebellion) ← ¹ Why do the nations rage

and the peoples plot in vain?

² The kings of the earth take their stand,

and the rulers conspire together

against the Lord and his Anointed One:

³ "Let's tear off their chains

and throw their ropes off of us."

⁴ The one enthroned in heaven laughs;

the Lord ridicules them.

⁵ Then he speaks to them in his anger

and terrifies them in his wrath:

⁶ "I have installed my king → *People (King David)*

on Zion, my holy mountain."

⁷ I will declare the Lord's decree.

He said to me, "You are my Son;   ⟶ *2 Samuel 7:14*
Mark 1:11
today I have become your Father.   *Hebrews 1:5*

⁸ Ask of me,

Promise ⟵
(Abrahamic covenant.)   and I will make the nations your inheritance

and the ends of the earth your possession.

⁹ You will break them with an iron scepter;

you will shatter them like pottery."

¹⁰ So now, kings, be wise;

receive instruction, you judges of the earth.

¹¹ Serve the LORD with reverential awe

and rejoice with trembling.

¹² Pay homage to the Son or he will be angry

and you will perish in your rebellion,

for his anger may ignite at any moment.

All who take refuge in him are happy.

In Christ, we find refuge.

Appendix C: Annotation Examples and Tips / 213

EXAMPLE ANNOTATION 3

Titus 2:14
Hebrews 9:15

Promise
(Redemption through faith in Jesus)

1 PETER 1:18–19

Problem (Sin)

Jesus's blood secures our redemption

[18] For you know that you were redeemed from your empty way of life inherited from your ancestors, not with perishable things like silver or gold, [19] but with the precious blood of Christ, like that of an unblemished and spotless lamb.

Theme (sacrifice)

Exodus 12
Isaiah 53:7
John 1:29

Highlight any words or phrases that point to Christ.

Make note of any attributes of God seen in the text.

Underline any words that point to the theme of sacrifice. Where else do we see this in Scripture?

Circle any words or phrases that show Jesus's connection to sacrifice.

The Metanarrative of Scripture

In order to see Christ in all of Scripture, this study makes connections between the Old and New Testaments each week. In order to understand these connections, it is necessary to read the entire Bible through the lens of the metanarrative of Scripture—the four-part, overarching story of the Bible.

CREATION

In the beginning, God created the universe. He made the world and everything in it. He created humans in His own image to be His representatives on the earth.

FALL

The first humans, Adam and Eve, disobeyed God by eating from the fruit of the Tree of the Knowledge of Good and Evil. Their disobedience impacted the whole world. The punishment for sin is death, and because of Adam's original sin, all humans are sinful and condemned to death.

REDEMPTION

God sent His Son to become a human and redeem His people. Jesus Christ lived a sinless life but died on the cross to pay the penalty for sin. He resurrected from the dead and ascended into heaven. All who put their faith in Jesus are saved from death and freely receive the gift of eternal life.

RESTORATION

One day, Jesus Christ will come again and restore all that sin destroyed. He will usher in a new heaven and new earth where all who trust in Him will live eternally with glorified bodies in the presence of God.

What is *the* Gospel?

Thank you for reading and enjoying this study with us! We are abundantly grateful for the Word of God, the instruction we glean from it, and the ever-growing understanding it provides for us of God's character. We are also thankful that Scripture continually points to one thing in innumerable ways: the gospel.

We remember our brokenness when we read about the fall of Adam and Eve in the garden of Eden (Genesis 3), where sin entered into a perfect world and maimed it. We remember the necessity that something innocent must die to pay for our sin when we read about the atoning sacrifices in the Old Testament. We read that we have all sinned and fallen short of the glory of God (Romans 3:23) and that the penalty for our brokenness, the wages of our sin, is death (Romans 6:23). We all need grace and mercy, but most importantly, we all need a Savior.

We consider the goodness of God when we realize that He did not plan to leave us in this dire state. We see His promise to buy us back from the clutches of sin and death in Genesis 3:15. And we see that promise accomplished with Jesus Christ on the cross. Jesus Christ knew no sin yet became sin so that we might become righteous through His sacrifice (2 Corinthians 5:21). Jesus was tempted in every way that we are and lived sinlessly. He was reviled yet still yielded Himself for our sake, that we may have life abundant in Him. Jesus lived the perfect life that we could not live and died the death that we deserved.

The gospel is profound yet simple. There are many mysteries in it that we will never understand this side of heaven, but there is still overwhelming weight to its implications in this life. The gospel tells of our sinfulness and God's goodness and a gracious gift that compels a response. We are saved by grace through faith, which means that we rest with faith in the grace that Jesus Christ displayed on the cross (Ephesians 2:8–9). We cannot save ourselves from our brokenness or do any amount of good works to merit God's favor. Still, we can have faith that what Jesus accomplished in His death, burial, and resurrection was more than enough for our salvation and our eternal delight. When we accept God, we are commanded to die to ourselves and our sinful desires and live a life worthy of the calling we have received (Ephesians 4:1). The gospel compels us to be sanctified, and in so doing, we are conformed to the likeness of Christ Himself. This is hope. This is redemption. This is the gospel.

GENESIS 3:15

I will put hostility between you and the woman, and between your offspring and her offspring. He will strike your head, and you will strike his heel.

ROMANS 3:23

For all have sinned and fall short of the glory of God.

ROMANS 6:23

For the wages of sin is death, but the gift of God is eternal life in Christ Jesus our Lord.

2 CORINTHIANS 5:21

He made the one who did not know sin to be sin for us, so that in him we might become the righteousness of God.

EPHESIANS 2:8–9

For you are saved by grace through faith, and this is not from yourselves; it is God's gift—not from works, so that no one can boast.

EPHESIANS 4:1–3

Therefore I, the prisoner in the Lord, urge you to walk worthy of the calling you have received, with all humility and gentleness, with patience, bearing with one another in love, making every effort to keep the unity of the Spirit through the bond of peace.

BIBLIOGRAPHY

Akin, Daniel L. *Exalting Jesus in Mark*. Christ-Centered Exposition Commentary. Nashville, TN: Holman Reference, 2014.

Andersen, Francis I. *Job: An Introduction and Commentary*. Vol. 14 of Tyndale Old Testament Commentaries. Downers Grove, IL: InterVarsity Press, 1976.

Beale, G. K., and D. A. Carson, eds. *Commentary on the New Testament Use of the Old Testament*. Grand Rapids, MI: Baker Academic, 2007.

Blum, Edwin A., and Trevin Wax, eds. *CSB Study Bible*. Nashville, TN: Holman Bible Publishers, 2017.

Bock, Darrell L. *Luke*. The NIV Application Commentary. Grand Rapids, MId: Zondervan, 1996.

Bromiley, Geoffrey W., ed. *The International Standard Bible Encyclopedia*. Revised. William B. Eerdmans Publishing Co., 1979–1988.

Calvin, John. *Commentary on the Book of Psalms*. Vol. 1. Translated by James Anderson. Grand Rapids, MI: Christian Classics Ethereal Library, n.d. https://www.ccel.org/ccel/calvin/calcom08/calcom08.i.html.

Chen, Diane G. *Luke: A New Covenant Commentary*. New Covenant Commentary Series. Eugene, OR: Cascade Books, 2017.

Davis, Andrew M. *Exalting Jesus in Isaiah*. Christ-Centered Exposition Commentary. Nashville, TN: Holman Reference, 2017.

Dial, Audrey, and Jennie Heideman, Helen Hummel, Alli McDougal, and Jana White, eds. *The Bible Handbook: A Book-by-Book Guide to the Entire Bible*. Spring, TX: The Daily Grace Co., 2024.

Gangel, Kenneth O. *John*. Holman New Testament Commentary. Nashville, TN: Broadman & Holman Publishers, 2000.

Keener, Craig S. *The IVP Background Commentary: New Testament*. 2nd ed. Downers Grove, IL: InterVarsity Press, 2014.

Kidner, Derek. *Ezra and Nehemiah: An Introduction and Commentary*. Vol. 12 of Tyndale Old Testament Commentaries. Downers Grove, IL: InterVarsity Press, 1979.

Kidner, Derek. *Psalms 73–150*. Vol. 16 of Tyndale Old Testament Commentaries. Downers Grove, IL: InterVarsity Press, 1975.

Lea, Thomas D. *Hebrews & James*. Holman New Testament Commentary. Nashville, TN: Broadman & Holman Publishers, 1999.

Martin, John A. "Isaiah." In *The Bible Knowledge Commentary: An Exposition of the Scriptures by Dallas Seminary Faculty*. Wheaton, IL: Victor Books, 1985.

Mohler Jr., R. Albert. *Exalting Jesus in Hebrews*. Christ-Centered Exposition Commentary. Nashville, TN: Holman Reference, 2017.

Morris, Leon. *The Gospel according to Matthew*. The Pillar New Testament Commentary. Grand Rapids, MI: William B. Eerdmans Publishing Co., 1992.

Morris, Leon. *Luke: An Introduction and Commentary*. Grand Rapids, MI: William B. Eerdmans Publishing Company, 1988.

O'Brien, Peter Thomas. *The Letter to the Hebrews*. The Pillar New Testament Commentary. Grand Rapids, MI: William B. Eerdmans Publishing Co., 2010.

Osborne, Grant R. *Colossians & Philemon: Verse by Verse*. Osborne New Testament Commentaries. Bellingham, WA: Lexham Press, 2016.

Patston, Kirk. *Isaiah: Surprising Salvation*. Reading the Bible Today Series. Sydney South, NSW: Aquila Press, 2010.

Smith, J. Josh, and Daniel L. Akin. *Exalting Jesus in Psalms 1–50*. Christ-Centered Exposition Commentary. Nashville, TN: Holman Reference, 2022.

Stott, John R. W. *God's New Society: The Message of Ephesians*. The Bible Speaks Today. Downers Grove, IL: InterVarsity Press, 1979.

Vroegop, Mark. *Dark Clouds, Deep Mercy: Discovering the Grace of Lament*. Wheaton, IL: Crossway, 2019.

Walton, John H., Victor H. Matthews, and Mark W. Chavalas. *The IVP Bible Background Commentary: Old Testament*. Downers Grove, IL: InterVarsity Press, 2000.

Webb, Barry G. *The Message of Isaiah*. The Bible Speaks Today. Downers Grove, IL: InterVarsity Press, 1996.

Youngblood, Ronald F., ed. *Nelson's New Illustrated Bible Dictionary*. Nashville, TN: Thomas Nelson Publishers, 1995.

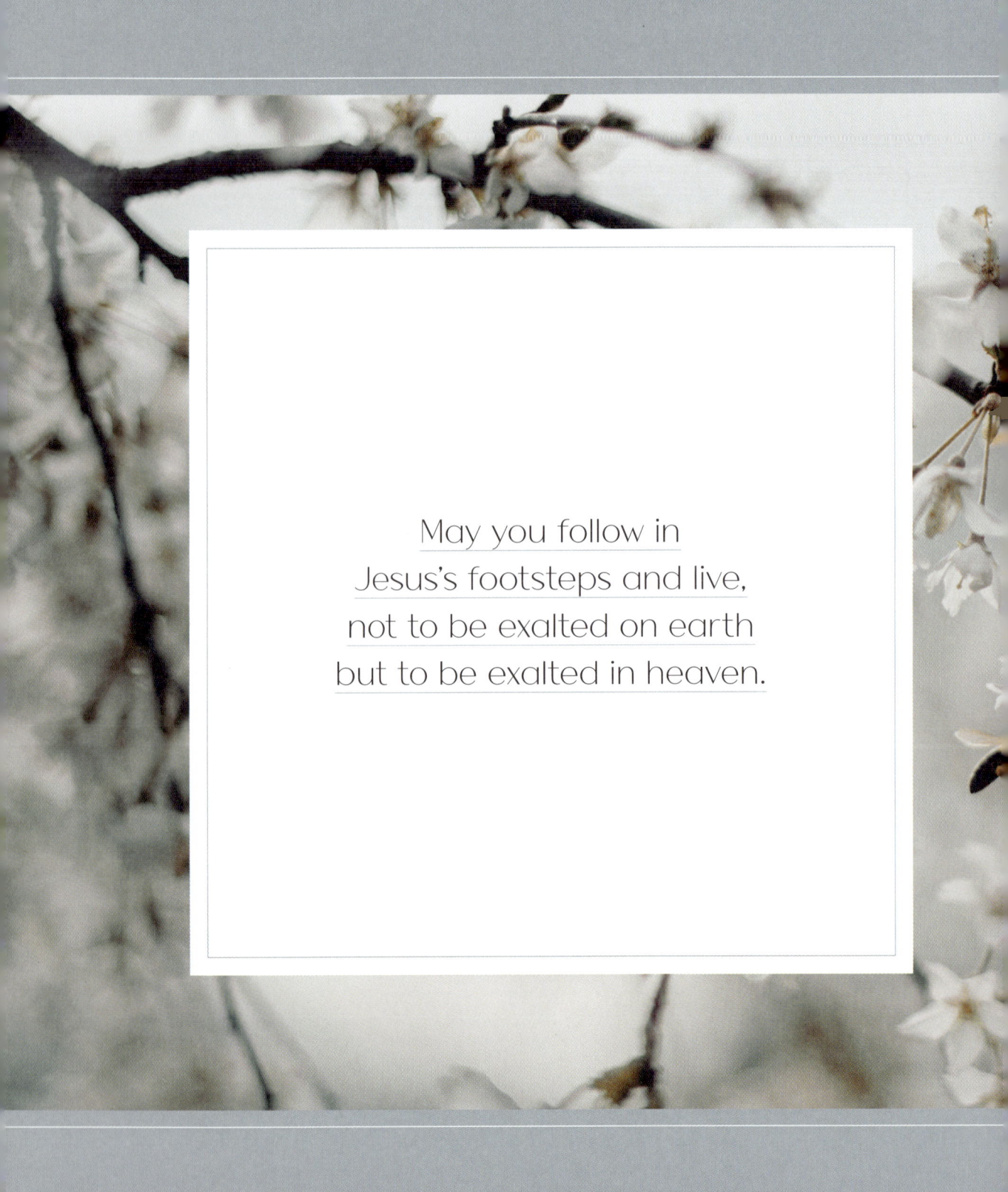

May you follow in
Jesus's footsteps and live,
not to be exalted on earth
but to be exalted in heaven.

Index

OLD TESTAMENT

Genesis
1:26–28	52
1:28–30	205
3	103, 216
3:15	167, 216, 217
3:16–24	52
6–9	204, 205
6:5	204
7:23	204
9:1–7	205
9:15–16	205
9:18–27	205
12:2–3	167
12:3	120
14	90, 94
14:1–16	90
14:16	95
14:18–20	90
15:5	28
49:10	95

Exodus
6:7	136
12–14	196
19:5–6	167
20–23	192
24	192
24:3	192
24:3–7	198
24:7	192
24:8	192, 197
29	90
32	103, 192

Leviticus
- 17.11 179
- 19:1–2 178
- 26:11–12 136

Deuteronomy
- 4:25–31 193
- 17:14–17 53
- 27–28 192
- 28 116
- 28:1–14 116
- 28:15–68 116

1 Samuel
- 8 53
- 13:14 78
- 19–30 64

2 Samuel
- 7:13 120
- 7:16 .... 120, 130
- 15–17 64

1 Kings
- 3:1–3 53
- 9:6–9 22

2 Kings
- 16:7–9 131
- 18:19–21 53
- 25:8–15 22

2 Chronicles
- 5:13 23

Ezra
- 1:1–4 23
- 3:10–11 .... 19, 20, 21, 22, 25, 28, 30

Job

1:12	37
1:20–22	33, 34, 35, 36, 37, 42, 44
2:4–6	37
2:10	37
28:28	100, 102
38:1	37
42:10–17	37

Psalms

2	212, 213
2:8	53
5	73
6	73
8	54, 56, 58
8:1–9	47, 49, 50, 51, 52
8:4–6	56
8:5	56
10	73
13	72, 73
22	61, 64, 66, 68, 69, 70
22:1	68
22:1–2	62, 63, 64, 68, 70
22:1–21	65
22:1–31	64
22:3–5	65
22:7	68
22:8	68
22:9–11	65
22:11–18	64
22:12	64
22:18	68
22:19–21	65
23	210, 211
44	73
80:8–11	124
86	73
88	73

Index / 223

110 .... 78, 79, 83, 90, 91, 92, 94, 95
110:1 .... 75, 76, 77, 78, 79, 80, 82, 84
110:4 .... 87, 88, 89, 91, 94, 95, 96
111:10 .... 100, 102
113–118 196
119:160 120
126 73
142 73

Proverbs

1:1–7 .... 100, 102
1:2 102
1:3 102
1:4 102
1:5 102
1:7 .... 99, 100, 101, 102, 103, 106, 107, 108
1:22 103
9:10 102
15:33 .... 100, 102

Isaiah

5:1–7 .... 111, 112, 114, 115, 116, 120, 122
5:2 121
5:2–4 122
5:5 117
5:5–6 113
5:7 .... 112, 113, 117, 124
5:8–16 117
5:12 117
5:16 117
6:13 131
7:1 130
7:1–9 .... 128, 130
7:1–17 130
7:10–14 .... 127, 128, 129, 134, 136
7:14 .... 132, 138, 139
7:15 131
7:15–17 128

7:18–25	131
8:9–10	131
9:6	53, 131, 205
9:6–7	134, 138
10	138
10:1–11	162
10:20–22	131
11:1	138
11:1–2	134
34:1–4	162
36–37	134
40:1–5	141, 143, 144, 145, 146, 152, 153, 154
40:2	146
40:3	153
40:4	142
40:5	147, 153
41–48	186
41–55	186
42:1	163, 186
42:1–4	163
42:1–9	186
42:6–7	157, 159, 160, 162, 163, 166, 167, 168
42:7	168
42:18–20	186
49:1–7	186
49:5	163
49:6	157, 158, 159, 161, 162, 163, 166, 167, 168, 186
50:4	187
50:4–9	186
50:6	138
52:13	138
52:13–15	173, 179
52:13–53:12	171, 172, 178, 180, 182, 184, 186
53:1–9	178
53:1–12	174, 175, 176, 177
53:2–5	138
53:3–12	43

Reference	Page(s)
53:5	138, 179
53:5–6	187
53:6	178
53:7	184
53:8	179
53:8–9	184
53:9	138
53:10–12	179
53:11–12	183
53:12	183
65:8–9	120

Jeremiah

Reference	Page(s)
1:4–8	192
1:17–19	192
1:18–19	192
2:21	125
11:1–17	192
11:7–8	198
25:1–14	192
27:1–15	192
28:1–4	192
29:4–9	192
29:10–14	23, 193
31:31–34	189, 190, 191, 192, 193, 194, 197, 198

Ezekiel

Reference	Page(s)
15:6–8	125
36:26–27	197

Hosea

Reference	Page(s)
1:11	205

NEW TESTAMENT

Matthew

1:1	134
1:1–25	134
1:19–20	134
1:21	134
1:21–23	127, 132, 133, 136, 138
1:23	135
5:16	30
16:21–27	69
22	82
22:41–46	75, 80, 81, 82, 84
22:43	83
26:17–30	42
26:36–46	33, 39, 40, 41, 42, 44
26:41	38
26:67	138
27:27–50	68
27:28–29	43
27:35	68
27:39	68
27:43	68
27:45–50	61, 66, 67, 70
27:46	68
27:51	29
27:57–60	138
28:1–10	69
28:16–20	69
28:18–20	135

Mark

10:35–45	182, 184
10:43–44	182
10:45	171, 180, 181, 182, 183, 184
15:15–19	138

Luke

1:17	152
1:32–33	138
1:41	152
2:32	167
3	152, 153
3:1–6	141, 149, 150, 151, 152, 154
3:2	149
3:21–22	141, 149, 151, 152, 154
3:22	153
22:1	196
22:1–23	196
22:7	196
22:8	196
22:11	196
22:13	196
22:14–20	189, 194, 195, 198
22:15	196
22:19	196
22:20	196
22:42	107
24:50–53	69

John

1:1	135
8:12	157, 164, 165, 166, 167, 168
9:6–7	166
9:35–41	166
10:10	121
10:14–16	28
12:32	138
15:1	124
15:1–5	111, 118, 119, 120, 122
15:1–17	121
15:5	121
16:33	44

    17:24 68
    19:25–26 43
    19:34 138

Acts
    2:32–33 197
    5:30–31 83
    13:47 167
    26:23 167

Romans
    3:23 .... 154, 216, 217
    5:3–5 44
    5:15–19 57
    8:1–4 197
    8:18 45
    8:34 83

1 Corinthians
    6:19–20 .... 29, 31
    15:45–47 57

2 Corinthians
    6:16 136

Galatians
    3:8 28
    3:27–28 28

Ephesians
    1:4–5 28
    1:11 28
    2:11–22 .... 19, 25, 26, 27, 28, 29, 30
    2:21 25
    2:21–22 30

Philippians
    2:3 184
    2:5–11 56
    2:7–8 184

  2:8 57
  2:15–16 30

Colossians
  1:1–2:1 104
  1:9 106
  1:9–10 106
  1:10 106
  1:12–14 106
  2:2–3 .... 99, 104, 105, 106
  2:2–10 106
  2:3 .... 106, 107, 108
  2:8 107
  3:1–3 107
  3:3 107
  3:5–17 109

1 Thessalonians
  5:11 30

Hebrews
  1:1–2 154
  2:5–9 .... 47, 54, 55, 56, 57, 58
  2:7–9 .... 57, 58
  2:9 54
  2:14–18 71
  4:15 44
  7 .... 92, 94, 95
  7:4 94
  7:11–17 .... 87, 92, 93, 96
  7:17 94
  7:22–24 95
  7:23–24 94
  7:27 95
  10:11–13 83
  12:2 .... 56, 96, 183

1 Peter
- 1:18–19 214
- 2:4–5 29
- 5:10 45

Jude
- 1:25 57

Revelation
- 5:9–14 58
- 21:3 30
- 21:3–4 136

Thank you for studying
God's Word with us!

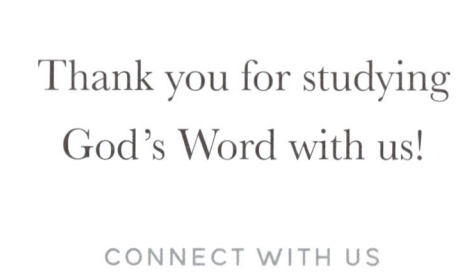

CONNECT WITH US
@thedailygraceco
@dailygracepodcast

CONTACT US
info@thedailygraceco.com

SHARE
#thedailygraceco

VISIT US ONLINE
www.thedailygraceco.com

MORE DAILY GRACE
Daily Grace® Podcast